# ABOLITION NOW!

## TEN YEARS OF STRATEGY AND STRUGGLE AGAINST THE PRISON INDUSTRIAL COMPLEX

T0163833

# ABOLITION NOW!

TEN YEARS OF **STRATEGY** AND **STRUGGLE** AGAINST THE PRISON INDUSTRIAL COMPLEX

THE CR10 PUBLICATIONS COLLECTIVE

Abolition Now!: Ten Years of Strategy and Struggle
Against the Prison Industrial Complex

by The CR10 Publications Collective

ISBN 978-1-904859-96-3

Library of Congress Number: 2008935483

AK Press
674-A 23rd Street
Oakland, CA 94612
www.akpress.org
akpress@akpress.org
510.208.1700

AK Press U.K.
PO Box 12766
Edinburgh EH8 9YE
www.akuk.com
ak@akedin.demon.co.uk
0131.555.5165

Design by Albert Ignacio and Marcelo Viana

*The CR10 Publications Collective is:*

*Ben Goldstein*
*Beth Richie*
*Craig Gilmore*
*David Stein*
*Dylan Rodríguez*
*Isaac Ontiveros*
*Jodie Lawston*
*Julia Sudbury*
*Michele Welsing*
*Rachel Herzing*
*Rickie Solinger*
*Yusef Omowale*

# CONTENTS

## SECTION 2: CHANGE

## SECTION 3: BUILD

# INTRODUCTION

From September 25–27, 1998, a conference, *Critical Resistance: Beyond the Prison Industrial Complex*, was held in Berkeley, California. The conference brought together nearly 3,500 people from around the world to examine a newly framed concept—the prison industrial complex (PIC)—and to explore the practical potentials of abolishing it. The convening not only provided a forum in which to foster conversations across organizations, locations, and sectors, but also re-ignited the fading spark of the anti-prison movement in the United States.

What no one knew during that weekend was what the lasting impacts of that conference would be. As rarely happens as a result of conferences, Critical Resistance (CR) jump-started pockets of organizing and strategizing around the US that would eventually merge and transform into the only national organization dedicated to the elimination of the PIC in the United States. Since that founding conference, CR has fostered chapters across the US and engaged in a wide range of projects and campaigns. Our work includes educational and leadership development projects with transitional housing for women and their kids, coalitional efforts to make choosing sites for and constructing new jails and prisons impossible, local campaigns to support people being released from imprisonment, and a generation of new materials and tools to help make PIC abolition more accessible.

Since 1998, some things have changed dramatically, while the steady drumbeats of caging and control remain consistently applied by those in power in the US as responses to everything from homelessness to immigration to gender non-conformity. The number of people serving time in US jails and prisons, for example, is substantially higher today than it was ten years ago. In 1998, about 1.8 million people were behind bars in US jails and prisons. Today, over 2.3 million people are imprisoned in US jails and prisons. And, while many were outraged by this year's Pew Charitable Trusts report announcing that more that 1 in 100 adults are imprisoned in the US, this number does not include the thousands caged in immigration detention centers, nor the thousands of young people locked in juvenile detention. Nor does it include more than five million people being formally surveilled through parole and probation. While the statistics highlight the enormity and the urgency of the situation, they can't tell the only story of the PIC's violence.

As we approach the tenth anniversary of the historic convening from which Critical Resistance was born, we are engaged in CR10, an anniversary organizing project through which we are assessing the past ten years of the movement against the PIC, the shifting context in which we work, and thinking strategically about how to be most effective in the years to come.

This book is part of a list of media projects developed by CR members and allies. Other media projects such as the films, *A Prison in the Fields: False Promise in the Central Valley* and *I Won't Drown on That Levee and You Ain't Gonna Break My Back*, and videos documenting the organizing from prior CR conferences, were created to foster political and intellectual engagement with the PIC. *Abolition Now!* is also situated within the lineage of other CR publications such as the re-print of *Instead of Prisons: A Handbook for Abolitionists*, a special issue of the journal *Social Justice* entitled "Critical Resistance to the Prison-Industrial Complex," and the quarterly newspaper *The Abolitionist*—a project of CR-Oakland. One of the many reasons publications are important is that they facilitate political dialogs between people who are locked up and those of us "on the outside." Such dialogs are central to our organizing strategy and our ultimate goals. We hope this set of dialogs will contribute to collapsing the separation between the "us" on the inside and the "us" on the outside. This process of abolition will make us all safer and healthier.

This publication also represents one method of assessment CR10 has provided us the occasion to use. One of the many focal points of CR10 is making PIC abolition central as both a strategy and the goal. We hope this book will contribute to that conversation. Its call, *Abolition Now!*, reminds us that there was abolition, there is abolition, and there will be more abolition. Likewise, as many organizers have demonstrated, we are not only struggling to tear down the cages of the PIC, but also to abolish the actions of policing, surveillance, and imprisonment that give the PIC its power. We are also reminded that abolition is the creation of possibilities for our dreams and demands for health and happiness—for what we want, not what we think we can get.

In this collection, we have compiled just a sampling of pieces to reflect the violent nexus of the PIC, and what abolition can look like. The collection is not meant to be exhaustive, but like CR10, to instigate a conversation and formulate strategy. We have compiled some suggestive pieces to reflect the many ways that PIC abolition presents itself. The book is guided by three sections that each reflect abolitionist practice: *dismantle, change, build.*

The first section, "Dismantle," is meant to assess the successes and challenges of the movement to abolish the PIC. "Perspectives on Critical Resistance" brings together the voices of sixteen CR members and allies to discuss struggles against the PIC. These are some of the many people who have, and continue to, breathe life into CR. INCITE! Women of Color Against Violence has also reflected on the important collaboration between INCITE! and CR, addressing the demand to link prison industrial complex abolition and the end of gender violence. Linking struggles, David Gilbert shows us the intimacies of imperialist statecraft, and how the US PIC is an articulation of warfare, while war is articulated in other forms throughout the world as well, be it in Iraq or Afghanistan, or the violence of neoliberal capitalism. Ofelia Cuevas demonstrates how the legacy of bearing witness to white supremacist violence is manifested both in the practice of lynching, as well as TV shows like *COPS*. Cuevas challenges us to question the ways that our vision is caught up in the "economy of punishment." Eddy Zheng's poem displays how part of the violence of the PIC forces us to live in different temporalities and consign certain people to premature death, while Jimi Marhsall's piece, "Black Burden," reflects on the pain created through a crucial piece of the PIC—anti-Black racism. Each of these writings reveals components of the brutal regime of the PIC; this process of identifying the PIC's articulations is central to our goals because, if we can't name what is killing us, we can't stop it.

Section two of the book, "Change," is intended to reflect some of the ways the PIC has adjusted and changed over the past ten years. As prisons are not the sole feature of the PIC, this section confronts the many tentacles of policing, surveillance, and caging—the raw materials for the PIC machine. The writings in this section relate dangerous trends in both expansion and mobilization of the PIC, and recount how some of those trends have been countered.

In "No One is Criminal," Martha Escobar shows how state terror through criminalization is a traditional practice of the US that has been deployed against Black and First Nations peoples. Escobar describes the importance of linking "immigrants rights" movements with struggles against the state terror of criminalization of all people. Pete White of the LA Community Action Network illustrates the increasing policing of Los Angeles under the "Safer Cities Initiative" (SCI). White shows how SCI has its historical grounding in the Black Codes of the post-slavery US South, and how "safety" is a term mobilized to repress low-capital communities and communities of people of color. Kim Pate expands our focus from the US state to show the symbiotic relationships between logics of imprisonment, policing, and surveillance in Canada and the US. Pate explains the insidious ways that patriarchy is deployed in the service of the global PIC. Pate also shows how many of the same strategies of "prison reform" being used for prison expansion in California are employed in Canada. Like Pate, long-time CR organizer Pilar Maschi explores the global PIC through the ways the "war on drugs" is deployed both intimately and politically. Maschi also shows how the practice of resistance is one strategy for surviving that war. Another long-time CR organizer, Dylan Rodríguez, suggests the political rhetoric of "warfare" is precisely the lens through which we must analyze the PIC. Like Maschi, Rodríguez calls out our obligation to survive and oppose this warfare.

Also in this section is the inspiring story of CR-NYC and the Community in Unity coalition, and their struggle against jail expansion in the Bronx. Here, CR-organizers and authors Rachael Leiner and Damien Domenack demonstrate how abolition is both the goal and the strategy for effective organizing. Alexander Lee of the Transgender, Gender Variant & Intersex Justice Project also shows the importance of creating more coalititional projects between activists and PIC abolitionists for the safety of transgender and gender variant people. Lee proposes movements based on demands for human dignity and asks to create more "prickly coalitions" between service-providers and anti-PIC activists. Similar to Lee's demand that abolition include our aspirations for the future, the poem "Can You Understand?," by Souligma Phothong, suggests compassion, love, and patience are some of the most necessary tools for enacting abolitionist practice. Such an analysis is crucial for us to reflect on as we attempt to live abolition each and every day, more and more.

The third section of the book, "Build," picks up where section two leaves off. The section focuses on the question: *what must we do to gain ground over the next ten years?* In her piece, RaeDeen Keahiolalo-Karasuda presents the historical context of the PIC in Hawai'i as it is used as a technology of colonial warfare against the Kanaka Maoli, Hawai'i's first peoples. In addition to showing how the PIC has been deployed against indigenous communities of Hawai'i, Karasuda discusses re-entry strategies for Kanaka Maoli that focus on "cultural literacy and political activism." Like Karasuda, Setsu Shigematsu, Gwen D'Arcangelis, and Melissa Burch, co-organizers of the Leadership, Education, Action, and Dialogue (LEAD) Project, discuss the political education programming that takes place at A New Way of Life, a group of transition homes for women coming home from imprisonment in the Watts District of Los Angeles. Through their experiences with the LEAD Project, Shigematsu, D'Arcangelis, and Burch display how "a politics of abolition can be practiced as part of this process of personal healing." Alexis Pauline Gumbs also suggests that abolition is not only smashing walls and cages but encouraging growth through the process of healing. Gumbs and the organizers of the UBUNTU coalition in Durham, NC, employ abolitionist strategies for responding to violence in a way that avoids reinforcing the PIC. Section Three closes with "Can You Hear." Written by a prisoner who must remain anonymous, this piece calls us all to struggle against the white supremacist state that constantly seeks to manage crisis through imprisonment and reform. This piece reminds us that our goal and strategy is *Abolition Now!*

This book would not be going to print without the dedication of many people. We wish to thank some of them for all their support throughout this process. To Molly Porzig, Nat Smith, Eric Stanley, Viet Mike Ngo, Ben Wang and the Asian Prisoner Support Committee, Charles Weigl, Jay Donahue, and rest of AK Press, thank you.

# SECTION 1:
# DISMANTLE

# PERSPECTIVES ON CRITICAL RESISTANCE

*Edited by Liz Samuels and David Stein*

In reflecting on the 10 years of strategy and struggle to eliminate the prison industrial complex (PIC) that has been the history of Critical Resistance (CR), we talked with people who have been involved in different phases of CR's organizational development. We asked them to offer their thoughts about CR's past, present, and future. What follows are excerpts from those conversations.

*How did you get involved with CR?*

ANDREA SMITH (AS): I was on the committee that organized the first Critical Resistance conference in Berkeley.

NANCY STOLLER (NS): I was invited to join the first steering/planning committee about a year before CR #1 at Berkeley. I joined the committee and did various jobs before and during the conference. After the conference, I was part of the collective that put out the special issue of *Social Justice*. [Vol. 27, No.3 (Fall 2000), "Critical Resistance to the Prison-Industrial Complex"].

JULIA SUDBURY (JS): I got involved with the planning committee for the first CR in 1998. At that time, I wasn't aware of the anti-prison movement in the US and I had only been in the country for a year. I learned about the histories of struggle here, as well as the contemporary conditions of incarceration and the rise of the PIC, through conversations with organizers during the conference and strategy session planning process.

**TERRY KUPERS (TK):** I was a member of the organizing committee for the first CR conference in Berkeley. It was thrilling to see so many committed, beautiful people come together, find out that we are not alone in our work and our vision, and team up to move the struggle forward.

**KAMARI CLARKE (KC):** Between 1997 and 1998, I was involved with the cultural component [of the '98 Conference]. . . . I got involved in that capacity—thinking about cultural expressions of freedom—as ways to think about questions of justice and to envision a different world. . . . [CR was] trying to understand how the PIC is developing, how things have changed over time, and how those on the inside and the outside might engage in different forms of expression that are relevant to survival.

**KIM DIEHL (KD):** I feel a little bit like a veteran and I can't really say that for many other organizations. I've been involved in CR since before CR had a presence in the South, and it has really changed the landscape of southern politics. [I'm] happy that that's happened because it's moved the prison industrial complex and southern politics to the forefront of our social movement in ways that maybe other issues haven't. People are really much more able to connect enslavement with prisons, or prisons with enslavement, and that the South has built a ton of prisons in the last 20–30 years. So, I think the history of CR for me as a Southerner is really big.

**TAMIKA MIDDLETON (TM):** I came to CR during the organizing for CR South. I had never really done any organizing before that. It was really a huge crash course in organizing, the PIC, abolition, and even New Orleans and the South, even though I'm a Southerner and had been in New Orleans for a couple years. The work was exhilarating. I felt so empowered! It gave me a new sense of myself, and a new outlook on the world in which I lived. I can say with all honestly that becoming a part of CR changed my whole world.

**ALEXIS PAULINE GUMBS (AG):** My first organizing project with CR was planning for CR East in 2000–2001. I wasn't involved in a sustained way. So in some senses CR10 program committee is my first real sustained organizing experience with CR.

**DYLAN RODRIGUEZ (DR):** My work with Critical Resistance has been the most humbling, mundane, and transformative political work in which I have ever engaged. I was a tiny part of the eighteen-month process of conceptualizing and organizing the first conference and strategy session at Berkeley in September 1998. … The first meeting of Critical Resistance was only a faint indication of what was to come. The initial ambition was to attract 400 people to a conference and movement-building session that would push—or, really, explode—the existing liberal and service-oriented frameworks through which organizations and individuals were essentially trying to manage, survive, and negotiate the prison industrial complex. The eventual turnout of 3,000-plus people at the first Critical Resistance conference and strategy session massively exceeded our wildest expectations and hopes, and I think it was no accident given that the tone and tenor of so many people at that 1998 event indicated that we were living in a moment of historical emergency that required new languages, new knowledges, new political labors.

**ARI WOHLFEILER (AW):** I first heard about CR from campus activists (students and staff) at UC Berkeley in 1999 who were involved in the third world Liberation Front (twLF) organizing effort to save the Ethnic Studies department from near total defunding and build a racial justice movement on campus in the post Prop 209 era (which ended Affirmative Action practices by the state of California). At that point, and I think this shows the incredible growth of the organization since the 1998 conference, I don't remember it being clear that CR was a membership or volunteer organization, whether it would continue to exist, whether it had campaigns, or what. It was just so much smaller than we are now. Rose, our first staffer, probably only worked part time then, CR East hadn't happened yet, and we hadn't formally figured out what type of organization we wanted to be.

*What would you like people to know about the history of CR and its role within social movements? What about the future of CR, following CR10?*

**ROSE BRAZ (RB):** Critical Resistance played a key role in re-invigorating what was a fairly dormant movement around prison issues. Moreover, CR pushed the debate and discussion from one that was very focused on reform to one that includes abolition as both a strategy and an end goal.

In 1998, while there were numerous people and organizations working around conditions of confinement, the death penalty, etc., and in particular using litigation and research strategies to fight what would be popularized as the prison industrial complex, grassroots organizing challenging the PIC was at a low following the crackdown on the movement in the 1970's and 80's. CR played a key role in building the grassroots movement that exists today by pushing the idea that a grassroots movement is a necessary prerequisite to change, and then bringing people

3

together through our conferences, campaigns, and projects toward the goal of helping to build that movement.

CR also has played a key role in altering the debate. Today, abolition is on the table, a goal that was not really on the agenda in 1998. A prerequisite to seeking any social change is the naming of it. In other words, even though the goal we seek may be far away, unless we name it and fight for it today, it will never come.

TM: CR South was a huge victory. Most Southern organizers that I know and have worked with will say the same. That was a huge breakthrough point in organizing against the PIC in the South. I think that the movement building and reframing that took place there was essential to the work, especially in the south where geography can make the work so isolated.

KC: [CR] pushed me to think about these mundane, everyday conceptions of justice, of prisons themselves, as if they do what popular culture thinks they do, as if they're meant to correct and help people. It pushed me in my own work and in my own teaching to get students to think more critically about those fictions in their lives and the implications as well as the ways that we're complicit in reproducing that fiction.

KAI LUMUMBA BARROW (KB): It's important for us to communicate with folks that we don't have answers; we are like everybody else, trying to figure out how to change the world. We have analysis, but not answers. We think our analysis is sound; it has historical roots and it's relevant to the direction that the world is moving, and where the world is currently in terms of the need to repress and control people. It's important to note that we are bold and that oftentimes when organizations are bold, there is a certain expectation that that organization or those people will lead us to freedom.

[Additionally] we are fun and creative, and we are trying to live abolition and that is challenging, and that means challenging and questioning and resisting as frequently as possible all the ways that we harm each other and the ways that we are harmed and the ways that we harm ourselves.

This is a really important moment for us to actually go back to the table and revisit some of the assumptions we've had for so long—and given the conditions and given the changes that are going on in the world, it's just time to seize that moment. I would love to see that happen at CR10.

**AW:** One thing that is so important about CR is that we have existed in so many different forms and have tried so many strategies in our short life. CR isn't an organization that spends hours and hours painstakingly perfecting every single thing we put out there, or zeroing in on one campaign or project with huge amounts of our collective resources. As a result, we've tried lots of different things in lots of different places with lots of different people. We have messed up and learned hard lessons and dealt with serious pain and loss all along the way, and that benefits us all in the end. But the range of our work really does show how hard we've worked to meet the PIC at every point: anti-expansion work, reading groups, legal services, parties, radio shows, copwatching, lobbying, political education, publishing, grassroots fundraising, bodywork and healing projects, letter writing with prisoners, housing and environmental justice organizing.

**BO BROWN (BB):** I'd like to see more street awareness come to the issue; I know we have to do all those things [legislative goals] and I know that it's much easier to do the legislative shit, and you get bigger feathers in your cap, but at some point I think it's really not about that. You have to do both. I think you can get lost in that and you can stay there and consider yourself a good person and never really get your hands dirty in a human kind of way. And I think that's not healthy. . . And I think working more with ex-prisoners in our little offices and in our little groups as much as we can. I'd like to see us come up with some kind of support group for families of prisoners that's real. We need to figure out how to support the prisoners when they're coming home. We need to understand post-traumatic shock on an ongoing, day-to-day basis.

**AS:** Many of the "restorative" justice models used as an alternative to prisons don't work when it comes to gender violence, and I often don't see prison abolitionists taking seriously concerns about safety for domestic and sexual violence survivors. Thus, I think it is important for prison abolitionists to focus on prison abolition as a positive rather than a negative project. That is, it's not simply about tearing down prison walls, but it's about building alternative formations that actually protect people from violence, that crowd out the criminalization regime.

**KB:** I would like to see us not be necessary anymore. I'd love to see us more rooted, not just in terms of community-based organizing, but to see more people who are directly impacted by the PIC more active in the organizing around it. I want to see us actively engaging each other more around the areas where we are challenged, both personally and politically. I want to see us be able to have honest

5

dialog and struggle, even though we might be afraid about hurting each others feelings, or being outcast … Everything I want to see for CR, I also want to see for our community, and I don't mean that just geographically. So, I want to see us being able to sit down and struggle together; I want to see us become more accountable to each other and define what that accountability means, to establish for ourselves a set of guidelines and principles that we can all agree to and change as we go along.

**AG:** I think CR is already up to this, but I really crave more nitty gritty details about what abolition looks like in people's daily lives. I am really excited about hearing more about community experiments … ways that people are replacing and outmoding cultures of punishment all the time.

**NS:** I think [US-based] abolitionists should study more how people in other countries are reducing their prison and jail populations. We should promote their strategies, explain how the fear of the other is reduced in other countries, and work more on fighting racism as a part of abolition work.

**TM:** I would really like to see more cultural work in CR. I think that young people and people of color outside of the progressive world understand the PIC in a very real way. What would it look like to talk about abolition to a sixteen-year-old Black boy who sets his watch to *106 and Park* and knows all the words to the latest Plies album? How do we reach out to artists like Plies who rhyme about the hardships of the system, but without making a political connection?

**VANESSA HUANG (VH):** My peers and comrades across a range of social justice movements share the vision and practice of developing accountability as a grounding point for our lives and political work, paid and unpaid. I think this speaks volumes to how we've centered the need to respond to and ultimately end the harms we face.

**RACHEL HERZING (RH):** We've done a good job at getting people with a myopic focus on imprisonment, even among abolitionists, to really think about the broader forces at work that make it possible to imprison people. It's been really important for us to articulate that and to have that always on our lips, because it keeps the entirety of the picture in focus. That's a huge challenge for us organizationally to manage, and we have a difficult time maintaining all of the different irons that we have in the fire at any given time, because this issue is so mammoth and ever-changing and interconnected and complicated. At the same time, it helps us make abolition more common-sensical to show the connections between all of these systems and practices and ideas, because people can always find a point of entry.

I want to see the movement to grow. I don't have an investment in CR becoming big or powerful. We're very low profile. I do have an investment in more people being open to abolition, as well as an investment for our allies to be able to work with us toward abolitionist goals.

TK: Litigation is important, of course, but not sufficient to make real change. There needs to be a loud public outcry for real justice, and that requires educating and organizing people. Of course, that's where CR plays a crucial role. Also, fear of crime in low-income communities is real. We need to speak to that fear in sensitive ways to bring more people into the movement for transformative justice. CR is in the frontline of those decrying the regressive trading away of liberties for an illusory sense of "safety," for example the Patriot Act and pre-emptive detention. Immigration lock-ups are some of the most abusive correctional facilities in the country. The struggle for transformative justice involves all the institutions of government and civil society, and I want to see CR continue and expand its links with others in the larger struggle.

RB: One big obstacle to abolitionist organizing is the erroneous belief by some that if you are an abolitionist, you don't care about conditions inside. In reality, nothing could be further from the truth. What is true is that as an abolitionist, I think the best way to improve conditions for people inside is to get them out.

I have seen CR's work become more coordinated, more sophisticated in employing multiple strategies and more challenging as the system has responded and adjusted to some of our successes. Most recently, we have seen our denunciation of conditions inside twisted by the state into justifications for expanding the system, particularly through what are sometimes called "boutique prisons."

What's new and more insidious about this expansion is that it has not been couched in "tough on crime" rhetoric that politicians usually employ to justify expansion. Rather, in response to growing anti-prison public sentiment, these plans have been grounded on the rhetoric of "prison reform" and, in regard to people in women's prisons, "gender responsiveness."

VH: We're now a part of emerging and overlapping conversations and movements that are building and growing who, what, why, how, and where we talk about and organize around gender, to begin to integrate gender self-determination and gender liberation frameworks and practices with existing frameworks challenging white supremacy and capitalism and patriarchy as critical to prison industrial complex abolition. Many of us have drawn tremendous lessons and inspiration from our organizing to found Transforming Justice, a national coalition supporting local organizing to end the criminalization and imprisonment of transgender and gender non-conforming communities.

JS: I would like to see us grow in developing a deep understanding of the need for healing as an abolitionist practice. Many of us come to this work with our own wounds, whether from childhood trauma, racism, homophobia, or the violence of police and prisons. In fact, many of us draw energy and inspiration from these wounds and the anger they create. But we also are drained by these traumas. Or we find ourselves neglecting our bodies and spirits in the same ways that we may have been neglected in the past. As a result, our movement can be very "head" oriented—talking, planning, thinking, writing—and not body and emotion oriented. This work doesn't have to be individualistic or separate from movement work; we can include it in all our movement spaces and make it a collective activity, just like the community recovery movement. But a movement against a violent and violating phenomenon like the PIC cannot hope to be successful if we don't directly address and heal the effects of that violence.

DR: It's both a tremendous obligation and honor to undertake the unfulfilled work of the best of our abolitionist precursors—those who did not only want the abolition of white supremacist slavery and normalized anti-Black violence, but who also recognized that the greatest promise of abolitionism was a comprehensive transformation of a civilization in which the sanctity of white civil society was defined by its capacity to define "community" and "safety" through the effectiveness of its ability to wage racial genocides. The present day work of CR and abolition has to proceed with organic recognition of its historical roots in liberation struggles against slavery, colonization, and conquest—and therefore struggle to constantly develop effective, creative, and politically educating forms of radical movement against the genocidal white supremacist state and the society to which it's tethered.

SHANA AGID (SA): I think [there] was a massive shift, whose initial foundation was created by [CR's] 1998 conference, that grew directly out of on-the-ground work and struggle to figure out work and engage with other groups doing work that ran counter to CR's mission—to not support any work that extends the life or scope of the PIC. That language was, not surprisingly, [a] risk, because really, that can be

8

almost any kind of reform. That was even more true in some ways ten years ago.

[Another] big shift in our thinking is guiding alternative means of both preventing and addressing harm and the conditions that make people so vulnerable to the system. I can absolutely see this in the kinds of sessions proposed for CR10. We've got at least five or six proposals dealing with the idea in innovative, contemporary, community-based, and grounded ways for CR10—both efforts underway and visions for learning more. I'm most excited by this.

**KD:** I think also with faith-based groups, we have more work to do, because a lot of faith-based groups benefit from prisons and I would like to see that shift in the next ten years. I would really like to see that change in the next ten years—have more radical work because that's what really moved slavery: when the churches started to take stands against it. And right now churches love going into prisons: all religions, except Judaism. I don't really hear a lot of Rabbis going over there.

CR has to make it clear that the priorities of our government are basically to increase "security" and not necessarily the quality of life for people.

**BB:** I'd like people to know that CR10 is able to happen after 10 years. And hopefully we'll be able to have at least 3,500 people here again—and more ex-prisoners. And I think, if you're in the prison abolition movement, if you're doing your job correctly, you have to intersect with other social movements—we cannot have tunnel vision.

*How does CR's work intersect with other organizing strategies and movements you are a part of?*

**KB:** The vast bulk of my organizing work has been specifically around political prisoners, so the obvious connection there is challenging the PIC as a space for halting dissent. I've also done a lot of work over the years around police violence, [and see] CR as a space for challenging the notion of policing in and of itself, not just around violence—police violence—but what gives this body of people an authority to control and militarize communities. And the third area, in terms of my work, is surrounding violence—sexual violence. Specifically, I've done work around violence against women, and that's included work around systems such as health care, systems such as reproductive freedom, as well as issues around interpersonal violence. How can we challenge how we harm each other, and how can we come up with different strategies for dealing with the way we harm each other and the ways that the state harms us? As a visual artist, I try to focus on representations, ideas, and commentary that focus on unleashing the imagination [and] on resistance, that attempt to encourage us to imagine different realities. For me, it's the values piece to Critical Resistance that's most important.

**AS:** I work on gender violence issues, where it is clear that the criminalization approach proffered in the mainstream anti-violence movement doesn't work. And, also, this criminalization approach obfuscates the role of the state in perpetrating gender violence. At the same time, we have to deal with the practical concerns for safety for survivors of domestic and sexual violence. Thus, we are working on developing community accountability strategies that do not rely on the state, and also do not depend on a romanticized notion of "community." This work goes to show the importance of developing alternative governance structures outside the nation-state system, of which the PIC is simply an arm. This intersects with work in indigenous rights movements, which have concepts of indigenous nationhood that are not based on nation-state forms of governance that rule through violence, domination, and control.

**KD:** I work for a union. I just left a meeting with some workers at Ft. Lauderdale airport, who are cleaners. They're almost all Haitian. Haitians here in Miami are almost all treated differently when they come here. For example, Cubans, once they hit land, [there is a policy] called "wet-foot-dry-foot" and they're completely able to become legal residents, but with Haitians, they are immediately put in detention, so that's a really big issue here. I just sat with a group of Haitian workers who face this everyday. There's always the fear of raids and that plays in with our organizing because a lot of people not only have fear about losing their jobs, but fear having their homes raided in the middle of the night and having family members taken.

I also have been staff and a volunteer for a queer youth center here. A lot of [the youth] come from families that are first generation here, that are immigrants, and mostly from working class, low-income communities of color. They're always coming to the center with stories about how the police harass them.

**AG:** Abolition provides a crucial challenge to how I work to respond to and end gendered violence against people of color in a way that really transforms our communities instead of locking us away from each other. Abolition provides an imperative for the anti-capitalist and economic justice work I do, because it reveals the costs of capitalism (a profound and deadly disconnection from ourselves and others epitomized by the prison industrial complex and the surveillance and policing state). I know that in order to have real safety we must have fair access to the resources we all need.

By centering the needs and the voices of the most impacted, CR provides a context and an infrastructure for the young people I teach (who are legally barred from public school property and mostly also on probation) to become organizers and warriors for their own freedom, which is what gives me hope every morning.

*What does prison industrial complex abolition mean to you?*

KD: It's a bold declaration. It's a tradition of stating the impossible, bring[ing] people along with a conception of how the world could be without slavery, without an economic system that just seems completely unbeatable—and permanent and static.

RH: Prison industrial complex abolition is dreaming wildly and having that be okay. It's genuinely asking for what we want, rather than what we think we can win. Why should I not want to be completely liberated and have my people around me and feel healthy and stable and be able to engage with people, to be able to hold people accountable?

RB: Abolition defines both the end goal we seek and the way we do our work today. Abolition means a world where we do not use prisons, policing, and the larger system of the prison industrial complex as an "answer" to what are social, political, and economic problems. Abolition is not just an end goal but a strategy today.

SA: It means facilitating and creating a kind of safety few of us have likely known, through self-determination and the capacity to struggle with each other and ourselves safely. Abolition of the PIC is, I think, about concrete struggle against the racial state in a political moment defined by a supposedly "post-racial" body politic, where race is theoretically less and less in evidence—and other groups of people, like the mainstream LGBT movement or immigrants rights movement, are banking on the notion that this is the mark of progress. Of course, race is not at all disappearing, except into the idea of crime and criminality, so that prisons and the PIC function as an articulation of racism that is, more or less, treated as inevitable or understandable. To struggle against this, I think, is to attempt both to work for lived lives and the people living them, and also to undo the "common sense" idea that the PIC makes sense of who belongs where and who deserves what.

AG: It means freedom now and day by day. It means accountability and love growing everywhere.

CONTRIBUTORS

ALEXIS PAULINE GUMBS is a queer, Black troublemaker. She works with Critical Resistance, SpiritHouse, Southerners on New Ground, and UBUNTU. She is also the founder of brokenbeautiful press (www.brokenbeautiful.wordpress.com).

ANDREA SMITH is the author of *Native Americans and the Christian Right: The Gendered Politics of Unlikely Alliances, Conquest: Sexual Violence and American Indian Genocide*, the editor of *The Revolution Will Not Be Funded: Beyond the Non-Profit Industrial Complex*, and a co-editor of *Color of Violence: The INCITE! Anthology*. She is a cofounder of the national activist organization INCITE! Women of Color Against Violence.

ARI WOHLFEILER is from Oakland, CA. He began volunteering with Critical Resistance in 2002. In 2006, he started working at CR doing fundraising.

BO (RITA D. BROWN) is a sixty-year-old white, working-class, butch dyke, anti-authoritarian prison abolitionist who has either been in prison or working to eradicate the prison industrial complex for the last thirty-five years. She is a proud member of All Of Us or None and regularly works with Out of Control: Lesbian Committee to Support Women Political Prisoners and the Prison Activist Resource Center, as well as many other abolitionist groups in the SF Bay Area and the world.

DYLAN RODRÍGUEZ is an Associate Professor at University of California-Riverside, where he began his teaching career in 2001. His first book, *Forced Passages: Imprisoned Radical Intellectuals and the US Prison Regime* was published in 2006 by the University of Minnesota Press. Among other political-intellectual collectives, he has worked with and/or alongside such organizations as Critical Resistance, INCITE! (a progressive antiviolence movement led by radical women of color, see incite-national.org), the Critical Filipino and Filipina Studies Collective (cffsc.focus-now.org), and the editorial board of the internationally recognized journal *Social Justice: A Journal of Crime, Conflict, and World Order*.

JULIA SUDBURY is an educator, activist, and writer who has been involved in the anti-racist, feminist, LGBT, and anti-prison movements in Britain, Canada, and the US for two decades. She is professor and chair of Ethnic Studies at Mills College in Oakland, and editor of *Global Lockdown: Race, Gender, and the Prison-Industrial Complex* (Routledge 2005). Julia is a founding member of Critical Resistance.

**KAI LUMUMBA BARROW** is the Training and Infrastructure Director with Critical Resistance, a national grassroots organization to end the prison industrial complex. Kai has been involved in social justice movements for the past twenty-five years. She has worked as an organizer and artist on issues related to prisons, policing, and gender violence, and emphasizes the intersections of race, gender, sexuality, and class.

**KAMARI CLARKE** was an original member of the Critical Resistance Steering committee and worked on the cultural integration of the arts component of the first Critical Resistance international conference, where she coordinated the musical, spoken word, visual arts, filmic, and general creative and performative components of the conference. With a Ph.D. in Anthropology and a Master of Law, today Clarke is an associate professor of anthropology at Yale University and research scientist at the Yale Law School, and continues to work on the intersections of social regulation, cultural notions of justice, and various forms of power. Over the past decade, Kamari has been the Yale faculty sponsor of the undergraduate support group for the incarcerated that provides mentoring support for incarcerated men and women.

**KIM DIEHL** is a founding member of Critical Resistance's National Organizing Body and helped launch CR South, held in New Orleans in 2003. She currently lives in her hometown, Miami, working in communications for the Service Employees International Union. She delights in writing at the beach, playing tennis year round, and returning her library books on time.

**NANCY STOLLER**, a research professor at University of California, Santa Cruz, is a long-time advocate for women prisoners and a researcher on health and healthcare in prison. She is currently the coordinator of the Jail and Prison Health Group of the American Public Health Association, and active in the World Health Organization's Health in Prison Project.

**RACHEL HERZING** is the CR10 Project Director at Critical Resistance.

**ROSE BRAZ** was part of the founding collective of Critical Resistance and currently is the Campaign Director for CR. Rose is on the board of Justice Now and the advisory board of California Coalition for Women Prisoners. Rose also comes to this work from personal experience supporting family members who have been in prison.

SHANA AGID is a writer, visual artist, and activist whose work challenges ideas of race, gender, and sexuality in the post-Civil Rights Era United States and reflects an investment in building new language to address new ideas and possibilities for undoing relationships of power in the 21st century. Shana has been working with Critical Resistance since 2000. Shana can be found/contacted at shanaagid.com.

TAMIKA MIDDLETON is a Southern woman of color, mother, and all around lover of the universe. Currently, she is pursuing a M.A. in sociology from Georgia State University. Critical Resistance has been raising her and her consciousness since 2002.

TERRY A. KUPERS, M.D., M.S.P. is Institute Professor at The Wright Institute, a Distinguished Life Fellow of the American Psychiatric Association, and, besides practicing psychiatry at his office in Oakland, he consults to various public mental health centers and jail mental health services. He provides expert testimony as well as consultation and staff training regarding the psychological effects of prison conditions, including isolated confinement in supermaximum security units, the quality of correctional mental health care, and the effects of sexual abuse in correctional settings. Dr. Kupers has published extensively, including the books *Prison Madness: The Mental Health Crisis Behind Bars and What We Must Do About It* (1999) and *Public Therapy: The Practice of Psychotherapy in the Public Mental Health Clinic* (1981). He is co-editor of *Prison Masculinities* (2002).

VANESSA HUANG is a queer, Chinese-American kid of immigrants from Taipei. Vanessa is the campaign director for Justice Now, an Oakland-based human rights organization that partners people in women's prisons with communities outside to build the movement for abolition, and organizes with Transforming Justice, a national coalition supporting local organizing to end the criminalization and imprisonment of transgender and gender non-conforming communities.

# THE CRITICAL RESISTANCE INCITE! STATEMENT ON GENDER VIOLENCE AND THE PRISON INDUSTRIAL COMPLEX

## INTRODUCTION

Ten years ago, Critical Resistance (CR) began with a bold mission of abolishing prisons, identifying the prison industry as a destructive, systematic, and persistent source of violence against oppressed communities. Yet CR's founding conference in 1998 was held during a moment in which much of the anti-violence movement found itself deeply entangled with police and prisons in the name of protection of survivors of rape and abuse. Instead of *resisting* prisons and policing because of the way this system creates, motivates, and reinforces rape and domestic violence both inside and outside of prisons, the anti-violence movement had developed a practice of *collaborating* with the state to increase police and prisons as a (frequently failed) means to increase safety for survivors of violence. (For a longer analysis of the anti-violence movement's relationship with prisons and police, please visit this webpage: http://incite-national.org/).

On the other hand, prison abolition efforts didn't exactly center the problem of domestic violence and sexual violence within the community. Calls for prison abolition were often not accompanied by recognition of the needs of survivors of domestic violence and sexual violence or the need for organizing efforts to ensure safety in the community *without* relying on police or prisons. Additionally, though survivors of rape and abuse often engage in criminalized survival activities that lead to incarceration, their experiences of violence both in the community and in the prison industrial complex were not necessarily reflected in prison abolition analysis. While many abolitionists rightfully acknowledged that prisons only reinforce the conditions that enable domestic and sexual violence, addressing the experiences of incarcerated survivors of violence and imagining and developing alternatives to prisons to address gender violence was not necessarily seen as fundamental to the politic of prison abolition.

Two critical political movements working in contradiction to one another, both marginalizing the experiences of women of color as well folks of color who identify as trans, two-spirit, or gender non-conforming. For the anti-violence movement, the normative survivor of violence was generally considered a white, heterosexual, middle-class woman who had no experience with violent policing or prisons and was not perceived as engaging in criminalized activity. For the prison abolition movement, the normative prisoner was generally considered a heterosexual man of color who did not necessarily experience violence within his community on the outside. Both political communities failed to see how the intersections of white supremacy, gender-based oppression, and other oppressions defined the way in which gender violence and incarceration mutually reinforce one another for *all* survivors and *all* prisoners.

In 2001, a group primarily consisting of women of color from Critical Resistance and INCITE! sat down for a weekend and created the *Statement on Gender Violence & The Prison Industrial Complex*. This statement turned out to be a vital organizing tool. It discussed the ways in which each movement was counterproductive to the other and, therefore, kept them from being as effective, creative, and powerful as they could be. The statement then recommended eleven concrete steps that each movement could take to transform the contradictory position between movements into a position of a *critically integrated politic*.

In the seven years since the CR-INCITE! *Statement on Gender Violence and the Prison Industrial Complex* first came out in 2001, a number of local and national groups and organizations have heeded its call and worked creatively and collectively toward making its vision a reality. The statement was widely circulated for signature through electronic, academic, and organizing communities, and disseminated on INCITE! and Critical Resistance's websites, and later, by way of colorful posters distributed by INCITE! It was published in a special issue of *Social Justice* journal, in *The Color of Violence: The INCITE Anthology*, published by South End Press in 2006, and most recently in INCITE!'s Organizing Toolkit to Stop Law Enforcement Violence Against Women of Color & Trans People of Color (available at: http://www.incite-national.org/index.php?s=52)

INCITE! is looking forward to taking the opportunity for reflection, learning from each other, and collective action presented by CR10 to share strategies, successes, and struggles in bringing the CR-INCITE! *Statement* to life. We also hope to further develop our analysis and action around the statement to more fully integrate and address multiple forms and experiences of state, interpersonal, and community-based violence.

We hope you will take a fresh look at the CR-INCITE! *Statement* in preparation for the conference, and join INCITE! and Critical Resistance in reflecting, talking, and learning during a pre-conference gathering on Friday September 25, 2008, throughout the conference, and beyond. The following questions will guide that discussion:

*Although the anti-sexual/domestic violence movements have been critical in breaking the silence around violence against women, these movements have also become increasingly service-oriented, professionalized, and de-politicized, and consequently are often reluctant to address sexual and domestic violence within the larger context of institutionalized violence and oppression. INCITE! recognizes that it is impossible to seriously address sexual/domestic violence against women and trans people of color without engaging in grassroots organizing efforts to challenge these larger structures of violence, such as militarism, attacks on immigrants' rights and Indian treaty rights, the proliferation of law enforcement and prisons, economic neo-colonialism, and the medical industry, and it is necessary to integrate a gender and sexuality analysis into these struggles.*

• How has the CR-INCITE! *Statement* changed the way we organize as abolitionists and anti-violence activists?

• How have we put the ideas in the statement into action?

• What challenges have we faced? What is holding us back from making the ideas in the statement a reality?

• What has worked, what hasn't?

• How have we documented state and interpersonal violence, ideas for community-based responses to violence, examples of movements working more collaboratively, and other strategies as part of our organizing work?

*Over the past decade, the prison industrial complex has not only expanded, it has widened its web through greater collaboration and complicity with the military, immigration enforcement authorities, law enforcement agencies, child welfare agencies, mental health systems, and social assistance agencies.*

• How can we better recognize, highlight, collaborate, and organize around:

▸ The role played by law enforcement as the front line of the PIC and police brutality and other forms of law enforcement violence against women and trans people of color?

▸ Increasing immigration and border enforcement violence, increasing collaboration between law enforcement and immigration authorities, profiling, criminalization and detention of immigrants, and violence against immigrant women and trans people of color?

▸ The links and overlap between the prison industrial complex and the military industrial complex in the US and overseas in terms of overall impacts of militarism and imperialism, as well as in terms of tactics, targets, and training?

▸ Understanding the prison industrial complex as encompassing multiple incarcerating institutions such as mental hospitals and disability institutions?

*The role of the prison industrial complex in enforcing the gender binary and gender conformity, along with systems of oppression based on racism, misogyny, and class, has become even more apparent as growing numbers of transgender and gender non-conforming people are subjected to violence in the criminal legal system, in large part as a result of discrimination in employment, housing, and virtually every aspect of society.*

• How can we better recognize, highlight, collaborate, and organize around:

▸ Gender violence against transgender and gender non-conforming people of color by police, within the PIC, in our communities, and in our homes?

*Criminalization and incarceration continue to be offered and pursued as means of achieving greater safety, particularly where domestic violence, sexual violence, and homophobic, transphobic, racist, misogynist, and religion-based violence ("hate crimes") are concerned.*

• How can we better recognize, highlight, collaborate, and organize around:

▸ Resistance to reliance on the PIC to address homophobic, transphobic, gender-based, racist, and religion-based violence ("hate crimes") and develop liberatory strategies for safety and accountability?

▸ The role in bolstering the PIC of legislation that purports to address gender violence (such as VAWA), homophobic, transphobic, gender-based, racist, and religion-based violence (such as "hate crimes" legislation), and prison conditions by making prisons "better" for people in women's prisons?

▸ Lack of protection from violence for Native women living on reservations, undocumented people, and sex workers and other criminalized women and trans people of color?

*Violence, criminalization, and incarceration of communities of color have been the default response to "disasters"—be they the September 11, 2001 attacks, the devastation wreaked by Hurricanes Katrina and Rita, or widespread poverty and despair in many communities of color.*

• How can we better recognize, highlight, collaborate, and organize around:

▸ The intersections of disasters, displacement, policing, and reproductive violence and population control policies?

▸ Law enforcement and prison violence and abuse during disasters; and how the state and mainstream media use disasters as opportunities to further criminalize, profile, police, commit acts of violence against, forcibly displace, and render invisible poor communities of color, particularly women, transgender, and gender nonconforming people, both in prisons and jails, and in the communities they once called home?

▸ The sensationalization of sexual and domestic violence during disasters by mainstream media to justify the use of law and order tactics of military personnel and law enforcements agencies to control, regulate, murder, and incarcerate people of color in the name of keeping women safe?

*Many of us have organized against sexual, family, and community violence and the prison industrial complex through non-profits. And many of us have been critically examining the "non-profit industrial complex" (NPIC)—the system of relationships between the state (or local and federal governments), the owning classes, foundations, and non-profit/NGO social service & social justice organizations—and the ways in which it results in the surveillance, control, derailment, and everyday management of political movements. The state uses non-profits to: monitor and control social justice movements; divert public monies into private hands through foundations; manage and control dissent in order to make the world safe for capitalism; redirect activist energies into career-based modes of organizing instead of mass-based organizing capable of actually transforming society; allow corporations to mask their exploitative and colonial work practices through "philanthropic" work; encourage social movements to model themselves after capitalist structures rather than to challenge them.*

• How can we better recognize, highlight, collaborate, and organize around:

▸ The relationship between the NPIC and PIC as it relates to the way state and foundation funding drives our political work, weakens critical coalitions, and undermines accountability to those most marginalized in anti-violence and prison abolition movements?

*The closing statement of the CR-INCITE! statement says: "We seek to build movements that not only end violence, but that create a society based on radical freedom, mutual accountability, and passionate reciprocity. In this society, safety and security will not be premised on violence or the threat of violence; it will be based on a collective commitment to guaranteeing the survival and care of all peoples."*

• What is meant by "radical freedom, mutual accountability, and passionate reciprocity?"

• Where have we been? How have we seen this statement embodied in the last 10 years? What kinds of language/strategies/ideas have been implemented to create real alternatives to law enforcement and the PIC that are rooted in caring, accountability and racial and gender justice?

• Where do we need to go? What kinds of movement building and organizing can help to fully bring this vision about?

• What kind of politics do we need to develop?

• How has the CR-INCITE! statement motivated stronger coalitions between multiple movements?

The Critical Resistance-INCITE! statement has proven to be a powerful tool to help initiate organizing strategies, legitimize radical women of color and queer people of color political analysis, and provoke creative out-of-the-box ideas for movement building. CR and INCITE! also work in collaboration with many other organizations and activists who are also pushing the envelope about potential cross-movement solidarities. The historic Transforming Justice conference in October 2007, for example, created a crucial opportunity to discuss and strategize around incarceration as it relates to violence against trans and gender non-conforming folks, gender policing, and poverty. Amazing local community-based organizations across the US (and abroad!) are also developing powerful ideas from critically engaging across movements, doing so by centering the experiences of folks on the margin who are articulating a necessity for this kind of cross-movement engagement and creativity.

It's a really exciting time! Radical social movements that we are building together are being challenged and pushed to incorporate critical and potentially movement-altering agendas and practices. Perhaps at the next ten-year anniversary, we will celebrate the ways in which these rich and transformative cross-movement collaborations have created unique and productive pathways towards liberation for all of us.

## THE STATEMENT

We call social justice movements to develop strategies and analysis that address both state and interpersonal violence, particularly violence against women. Currently, activists/movements that address state violence (such as anti-prison, anti-police brutality groups) often work in isolation from activists/movements that address domestic and sexual violence. The result is that women of color, who suffer disproportionately from both state and interpersonal violence, have become marginalized within these movements. It is critical that we develop responses to gender violence that do not depend on a sexist, racist, classist, and homophobic criminal justice system. It is also important that we develop strategies that challenge the criminal justice system and that also provide safety for survivors of sexual and domestic violence. To live violence-free lives, we must develop holistic strategies for addressing violence that speak to the intersection of all forms of oppression.

The anti-violence movement has been critically important in breaking the silence around violence against women and providing much-needed services to survivors. However, the mainstream anti-violence movement has increasingly relied on the criminal justice system as the front-line approach toward ending violence against women of color. It is important to assess the impact of this strategy.

1 Law enforcement approaches to violence against women may deter some acts of violence in the short term. However, as an overall strategy for ending violence, criminalization has not worked. In fact, the overall impact of mandatory arrest laws for domestic violence have led to decreases in the number of battered women who kill their partners in self-defense, but they have not led to a decrease in the number of batterers who kill their partners. Thus, the law protects batterers more than it protects survivors.

2 The criminalization approach has also brought many women into conflict with the law, particularly women of color, poor women, lesbians, sex workers, immigrant women, women with disabilities, and other marginalized women. For instance, under mandatory arrest laws, there have been numerous incidents where police officers called to domestic incidents have arrested the woman who is being

battered.[1] Many undocumented women have reported cases of sexual and domestic violence, only to find themselves deported.[2] A tough law-and-order agenda also leads to long punitive sentences for women convicted of killing their batterers.[3] Finally, when public funding is channeled into policing and prisons, budget cuts for social programs, including women's shelters, welfare, and public housing are the inevitable side-effect.[4] These cutbacks leave women less able to escape violent relationships.

3 Prisons don't work. Despite an exponential increase in the number of men in prisons, women are not any safer, and the rates of sexual assault and domestic violence have not decreased.[5] In calling for greater police responses to and harsher sentences for perpetrators of gender violence, the anti-violence movement has fueled the proliferation of prisons which now lock up more people per capita in the US than any other country.[6] During the past fifteen years, the numbers of women, especially women of color in prison has skyrocketed.[7] Prisons also inflict violence on the growing numbers of women behind bars. Slashing, suicide, the proliferation of HIV, strip searches, medical neglect, and rape of prisoners has largely been ignored by anti-violence activists.[8] The criminal justice system, an institution of violence, domination, and control, has increased the level of violence in society.

4 The reliance on state funding to support anti-violence programs has increased the professionalization of the anti-violence movement and alienated it from its community-organizing, social justice roots.[9] Such reliance has isolated the anti-violence movement from other social justice movements that seek to eradicate state violence, such that it acts in conflict rather than in collaboration with these movements.

5 The reliance on the criminal justice system has taken power away from women's ability to organize collectively to stop violence and has invested this power within the state. The result is that women who seek redress in the criminal justice system feel disempowered and alienated.[10] It has also promoted an individualistic approach toward ending violence such that the only way people think they can intervene in stopping violence is to call the police. This reliance has shifted our focus from developing ways communities can collectively respond to violence.

In recent years, the mainstream anti-prison movement has called attention to the negative impact of criminalization and the build-up of the prison industrial complex. Because activists seeking to reverse the tide of mass incarceration and criminalization of poor communities and communities of color have not always centered gender and sexuality in their analysis or organizing, we have not always responded adequately to the needs of survivors of domestic and sexual violence.

1 Prison and police accountability activists have generally organized around and conceptualized men of color as the primary victims of state violence.[11] Women prisoners and victims of police brutality have been made invisible by a focus on the war on our brothers and sons. It has failed to consider how women are affected as severely by state violence as men.[12] The plight of women who are raped by INS officers or prison guards, for instance, has not received sufficient attention. In addition, women carry the burden of caring for extended family when family and community members are criminalized and warehoused.[13] Several organizations have been established to advocate for women prisoners;[14] however, these groups have been frequently marginalized within the mainstream anti-prison movement.

2 The anti-prison movement has not addressed strategies for addressing the rampant forms of violence women face in their everyday lives, including street harassment, sexual harassment at work, rape, and intimate partner abuse. Until these strategies are developed, many women will feel shortchanged by the movement. In addition, by not seeking alliances with the anti-violence movement, the anti-prison movement has sent the message that it is possible to liberate communities without seeking the well-being and safety of women.

3 The anti-prison movement has failed to sufficiently organize around the forms of state violence faced by Lesbian, Gay, Bisexual, Trans, Twospirited, and Intersex (LGBTTI) communities. LGBTTI street youth and trans people in general are particularly vulnerable to police brutality and criminalization.[15] LGBTTI prisoners are denied basic human rights such as family visits from same sex partners, and same sex consensual relationships in prison are policed and punished.[16]

4 While prison abolitionists have correctly pointed out that rapists and serial murderers comprise a small number of the prison population, we have not answered the question of how these cases should be addressed.[17] The inability to answer the question is interpreted by many anti-violence activists as a lack of concern for the safety of women.

5 The various alternatives to incarceration that have been developed by anti-prison activists have generally failed to provide sufficient mechanisms for safety and accountability for survivors of sexual and domestic violence. These alternatives often rely on a romanticized notion of communities, which have yet to demonstrate their commitment and ability to keep women and children safe, or seriously address the sexism and homophobia that is deeply embedded within them.[18]

We call on social justice movements concerned with ending violence in all its forms to:

1 Develop community-based responses to violence that do not rely on the

criminal justice system AND which have mechanisms that ensure safety and accountability for survivors of sexual and domestic violence. Transformative practices emerging from local communities should be documented and disseminated to promote collective responses to violence.

2 Critically assess the impact of state funding on social justice organizations and develop alternative fundraising strategies to support these organizations. Develop collective fundraising and organizing strategies for anti-prison and anti-violence organizations. Develop strategies and analysis that specifically target state forms of sexual violence.

3 Make connections between interpersonal violence, the violence inflicted by domestic state institutions (such as prisons, detention centers, mental hospitals, and child protective services), and international violence (such as war, military base prostitution, and nuclear testing).

4 Develop an analysis and strategies to end violence that do not isolate individual acts of violence (either committed by the state or individuals) from their larger contexts. These strategies must address how entire communities of all genders are affected in multiple ways by both state violence and interpersonal gender violence. Battered women prisoners represent an intersection of state and interpersonal violence and as such provide and opportunity for both movements to build coalitions and joint struggles.

5 Put poor/working class women of color in the center of their analysis, organizing practices, and leadership development. Recognize the role of economic oppression, welfare "reform," and attacks on women workers' rights in increasing women's vulnerability to all forms of violence and locate anti-violence and anti-prison activism alongside efforts to transform the capitalist economic system.

6 Center stories of state violence committed against women of color in our organizing efforts.

7 Oppose legislative change that promotes prison expansion, criminalization of poor communities and communities of color and thus state violence against women of color, even if these changes also incorporate measures to support victims of interpersonal gender violence.

8 Promote holistic political education at the everyday level within our communities, specifically how sexual violence helps reproduce the colonial, racist, capitalist, heterosexist, and patriarchal society we live in, as well as how state violence produces interpersonal violence within communities.

9 Develop strategies for mobilizing against sexism and homophobia WITHIN our communities in order to keep women safe.

10 Challenge men of color and all men in social justice movements to take par-

ticular responsibility to address and organize around gender violence in their communities as a primary strategy for addressing violence and colonialism. We challenge men to address how their own histories of victimization have hindered their ability to establish gender justice in their communities.

11 Link struggles for personal transformation and healing with struggles for social justice.

We seek to build movements that not only end violence, but that create a society based on radical freedom, mutual accountability, and passionate reciprocity. In this society, safety and security will not be premised on violence or the threat of violence; it will be based on a collective commitment to guaranteeing the survival and care of all peoples.

Signatures:

**ORGANIZATIONS**

American Friends Service Committee
Arizona Prison Moratorium Coalition
Audre Lorde Project
California Coalition for Women Prisoners
Center for Human Rights Education
Center for Immigrant Families
Center for Law and Justice
Colorado Progressive Alliance
Committee Against Anti-Asian Violence (New York)
Communities Against Rape and Abuse (Seattle)
Direct Action Against Refugee Exploitation (Vancouver)
Institute of Lesbian Studies
Justice Now
Korean American Coalition to End Domestic Abuse
Legal Services for Prisoners with Children
Minnesota Black Political Action Committee
National Coalition Against Domestic Violence
Northwest Immigrant Rights Project (Seattle)
Pennsylvania Lesbian and Gay Task Force
Prison Activist Resource Center
Project South

San Francisco Women Against Rape
SHIMTUH Korean Domestic Violence Program
Sista II Sista
Southwest Youth Collaborative (Chicago)
Spear and Shield Publications, Chicago
Women of All Red Nations
Women of Color Resource Center
Youth Ministries for Peace and Justice (Bronx)

INCITE! WOMEN OF COLOR AGAINST VIOLENCE *is a national activist organiza-*
*tion of radical feminists of color advancing a movement to end violence against*
*women of color and our communities through direct action, critical dialog, and*
*grassroots organizing.*

CRITICAL RESISTANCE *is a national grassroots organization committed to end-*
*ing society's use prisons and policing as an answer to social problems.*

**NOTES**

1   See Martha McMahon, "Making Social Change," *Violence Against Women* 9, no. 1 (January 2003):
47-74; Sue Osthoff, "But Gertrude, I Beg to Differ, a Hit is Not a Hit is Not a Hit," *Violence Against
Women* 8, no. 12 (December 2002): 1521-1544; Susan Miller, "The Paradox of Women Arrested for Domestic Violence," *Violence Against Women* 7, no. 12 (December 2001). Noting that in some cities, over
20% of those arrested for domestic violence are women, Miller concludes: "An arrest policy intended
to protect battered women as victims is being misapplied and used against them. Battered women
have become female offenders."

2   Women's dependent or undocumented status is often manipulated by batterers, who use the
threat of deportation as part of a matrix of domination and control. Although the Violence Against
Women Act (VAWA 1994 and 2000) introduced visas for battered immigrant women, many women
do not know about the act's provisions or are unable to meet evidentiary requirements. Since the
Illegal Immigration Reform and Immigrant Responsibility Act made domestic violence grounds for
deportation, women may also be reluctant to subject a legal permanent resident spouse to potential
deportation proceedings by reporting him to the police. In addition, women arrested under mandatory arrest laws could themselves face deportation. See Anita Raj and Jay Silverman, "Violence Against
Immigrant Women: The Role of Culture, Context, and Legal Immigrant Status on Intimate Partner

Violence," *Violence Against Women* 8, no. 3 (March 2002), 367-398. Deena Jang, Len Marin, and Gail Pendleton, *Domestic Violence in Immigrant and Refugee Communities: Assessing the Rights of Battered Women*, 2nd Edition, San Francisco: Family Violence Prevention Fund, 1997.

3    For example, California Governor Grey Davis, whose tough law-and-order platform included a promise that no one convicted of murder would go free, has rejected numerous parole board recommendations on behalf of battered women incarcerated for killing in self defense. Rebecca Vesely, "Davis' Right to Deny Parole to Abused Women Upheld," *Women's Enews*, December 19, 2002. For further information and testimonies of incarcerated survivors of domestic violence, see www.freebatteredwomen.org.

4    Christian Parenti documents the shift in government spending from welfare, education, and social provision to prisons and policing in *Lockdown America: Policing and Prisons in the Age of Crisis*, London: Verso Books, 1999.

5    The US prison and jail population grew from 270,000 in 1975 to two million in 2001 as legislators pushed "tough on crime" policies such as mandatory minimums, three-strikes-and-you're out, and truth in sentencing (Michael Tonry, *Penal Reform in Overcrowded Times*, Oxford: Oxford University Press, 2001: 17). Over 90% of these prisoners are men, and approximately 50% are black men. Despite claims that locking more people away would lead to a dramatic decrease in crime, reported violent crimes against women have remained relatively constant since annual victimization surveys were initiated in 1973. Bureau of Justice Statistics, National Crime Victimization Survey Report: "Violence Against Women", NCJ 145325, 1994.

6    In 2001, the US, with 686 prisoners per 100,000 residents surpassed the incarceration rate of gulag-ridden Russia. The US dwarfs the incarceration rate of Western European nations like Finland and Denmark, which incarcerate only 59 people in every 100,000. Home Office Development and Statistics Directorate, *World Prison Population List*, 2003. Available at: www.homeoffice.gov.uk/rds/pdfs2/r188.pdf.

7    The rate of increase of women's imprisonment in the US has exceeded that of men. In 1970, there were 5,600 women in federal and state prisons, by 1996 there were 75,000 (Elliot Currie, *Crime and Punishment in America*, New York: Henry Holt, 1998).

8    Amnesty International's investigation of women's prisons in the US revealed countless cases of sexual, physical, and psychological abuse. In one case, the Federal Bureau of Prisons paid $500,000 to settle a lawsuit by three black women who were sexually assaulted when guards took money from male prisoners in exchange for taking them to the women's cells; prisoners in Arizona were subjected to rape, sexual fondling, and genital touching during searches as well as constant prurient viewing when using the shower and toilet; women at Valley State Prison, California, were treated as a "private harem to sexually abuse and harass"; in numerous cases, women were kept in restraints while seriously ill, dying, or in labor, and women under maximum security conditions were kept in isolation and sensory deprivation for long periods. *Not Part of My Sentence: Violations of the Human Rights of Women in Custody*, 1999.

9    Andrea Smith, "Colors of Violence," *Colorlines* 3, no. 4 (2000-2001).

10   May Koss argues that the adversarial justice system traumatizes survivors of domestic violence. "Blame, Shame and Community: Justice Responses to Violence Against Women," *American Psychologist* 55, no. 11 (November 2000): 1332. For a first-person account of a rape survivor's fight to hold the police accountable see *The Story of Jane Doe: A Book About Rape*, New York: Random House, 2003. Jane Doe was raped by the Toronto "balcony rapist" after police used women in her neighborhood as "bait."

11   Beth Richie, "The Social Impact of Mass Incarceration on Women," in *Invisible Punishment: The Collateral Consequences of Mass Imprisonment*, edited by Marc Mauer and Meda Chesney-Lind, New York: New Press, 2002.

12   For a comprehensive account of state violence against women in the US, see Annanya Bhattacharjee, *Women of Color and the Violence of Law Enforcement*, Philadelphia: American Friends Service Committee and Committee on Women, Population, and the Environment, 2001.

13   Additional burdens on women when a loved one is incarcerated include dealing with the arrest and trials of family members, expensive visits and phone calls from correctional facilities, and meeting disruptive parole requirements (Richie 2002).

14   In the US, see Justice Now; Legal Services for Prisoners with Children http://prisonerswith children.org; Free Battered Women www.freebatteredwomen.org; California Coalition for Women Prisoners http://womenprisoners.org; Chicago Legal Advocacy for Incarcerated Mothers www.c-l-a-i-m-.org. In the UK, see Women in Prison www.womeninprison.org; Justice for Women www.jfw. org.uk. In Canada, see the Canadian Association of Elizabeth Fry Associations www.elizabethfry.ca/caefs_e.htm.

15   According to transgender activists in the Bay Area, the police are responsible for approximately 50% of all trans abuse cases. The Transaction hotline regularly receives reports from TG/TS survivors of police violence who have been forced to strip in order to "verify gender," or subjected to demands for sex from undercover police officers. "Transgender Sues Police," *San Francisco Examiner*, August 9, 2002; "Another Transgender Murder," *Bay Area Reporter*, April 8, 1999.

16   Karlene Faith, *Unruly Women: The Politics of Confinement and Resistance*. Vancouver: Press Gang Publishers, 1993.

17   Abolitionists Thomas and Boehlfeld's response to the question: "What Do We Do with Henry?" where Henry is a violent rapist, is an example of this problem. The authors conclude that this is the wrong question since it focuses attention on a small and anomalous subsection of the prison population and detracts from a broader abolitionist vision (Jim Thomas and Sharon Boehlefeld, "Rethinking Abolitionism: 'What Do We Do with Henry?'" in *We Who Would Take No Prisoners: Selections From the Fifth International Conference on Penal Abolition*, edited by Brian MacLean and Harold Pepinsky, Vancouver: Collective Press, 1993).

18   Alternatives to the traditional justice system such as Sentencing Circles are particularly developed in Canada and Australia, where they have been developed in partnership with indigenous communities. However, native women have been critical of these approaches, arguing that they fail

to address the deep-rooted sexism and misogyny engendered by experiences of colonization and that they may revictimize women (Patricia Monture-Angus, "The Roles and Responsibilities of Aboriginal Women: Reclaiming justice," in *Criminal Injustice: Racism in the Criminal Justice System*, edited by Robynne Neugebauer, Toronto: Canadian Scholars' Press Inc., 2000). See also, Barbara Hudson, "Restorative Justice and Gendered Violence," *British Journal of Criminology* 42, no. 3 (Summer 2002).

# A SYSTEM WITHIN THE SYSTEM: THE PRISON INDUSTRIAL COMPLEX AND IMPERIALISM

*David Gilbert*

For those of us held behind locked gates within the walls and fences topped with razor wire, the "corrections" regime is the system that works tirelessly to impose total control over every aspect of our lives. Yet as ponderous and powerful as prisons are, they're only one part, a central girder, of a much bigger and more foreboding house of horrors which can be most accurately named "imperialism." The structural needs of the larger edifice set the specifications for the size and position of the girder; the strength of the girder helps determine how long the building will stand. We can't understand the explosion of imprisonment in the US since 1971 without looking at imperialism's urgent needs and goals of the period. By the same token, we can't develop an effective program around the prison industrial complex, without grappling with the stresses and trends of the larger system of imperial rule.

To be clear, before you take time to read this paper, I don't offer any brilliant ideas on strategy; those will most likely emerge from the organizing and activist efforts themselves. However, some of the concerns discussed may raise questions that go into forming strategy. I definitely look forward to learning from the dialogs that CR-10 generates on these issues.

## NAMING THE SYSTEM

"Imperialism" may sound like the kind of rhetoric we want to avoid, but it's one word that needs to be rescued as the best way to name the system that rules over us. The basis of imperialism is the relentless quest for profits around the globe. Its most striking characteristic is the colossal and grotesque polarization of wealth. That polarization happens between nations, between the rich countries of the North and the impoverished ones of the global South, the impoverished countries of Africa, Latin America, and parts of Asia; and at the same time within each country based on class, race and gender. The poles of dazzling wealth and abject poverty are intimately linked, as the former results from the ruthless plunder of the latter.

This system is built on and intensifies all the major forms of oppression: patriarchy, capitalism, and white supremacy, all of which are structurally central. At the same time, "imperialism" highlights the global character of the system in a way that explains why the most intense oppression and resistance have been in the South and that also provides the context for why the liberation struggles of the various peoples of color have been in the forefront within the US.

There is no way to capture what this system costs in human life and potential, the pain and the loss for all of us. Close to one billion human beings suffer chronic hunger, while another two billion face nutritional deficiencies; one billion lack access to clean drinking water. Just looking at children under the age of five, imperialism is a holocaust in progress: over 9 million die each year from easily preventable causes associated with poverty. The price for future generations may be even more severe as the rapaciousness of this global frenzy for profits threatens the very ecological basis for sustaining human life of any scale.

Since most people won't accept living in squalor amid plenty, imperialism entails both the most sophisticated and the most brutal forms of social control. Its most salient feature is war, war after war after war, mainly against the peoples of the South. The domestic front-line of such repression is a truly violent and harmful prison industrial complex.

## STRUCTURAL CRISIS AND PRISON EXPANSION

Today, 2,300,000 are held behind bars, about seven times the number in 1971. That explosion was unprecedented, coming after a seventy year period when the rates of imprisonment had remained more or less constant. This dramatic change did not result from some sudden skyrocketing of criminal activity but rather from a radical expansion of what was designated as a crime and a draconian increase in the punishments. Such extreme measures were driven by considerations way beyond "criminal justice" and often at cross purposes to the proclaimed goal of "public safety."

These destructive changes were born from crisis, one much more severe and protracted than the periodic ups and downs of the business cycles that occur over a roughly ten year period, but rather a situation that threatened the very survival of the system. Such structural crises occur because capitalism is by its nature unstable;

the economy is vast and complicated but the major decisions are made by a tiny corporate and financial elite, with each thinking only of his own profits. When a structural crisis develops, the long-term institutional arrangements that assured a reliable flow of profits and the rule of capital no longer function.

One dramatic example was the Great Depression of the 1930s, followed by World War II. At the end of that period a new set of international institutions, such as the International Monetary Fund (IMF) and the World Bank (WB), were created. At the same time, a new deal was hammered out for the terms of the bargain between capital and labor within the US. Those arrangements worked well for capital until they broke down a generation later. That new structural crisis, which emerged between 1968 and 1973, is the seedbed for the burgeoning of the prison industrial complex and many related changes in US society.

The first and most obvious signs were political, as the resistance to imperialism crested in 1968. The Vietnamese were defeating what had been seen as the US military juggernaut, and national liberation struggles raged throughout the third world. Bogged down abroad, the rulers faced the daunting prospect of a two-front war as 125 cities at home erupted with ghetto uprisings. Militant liberation movements surged among other peoples of color within the US. These struggles inspired a series of other challenges to the system: antiwar youth became increasingly radical; the women's liberation movement caught fire; a new environmental awareness emerged.

These upheavals combined to hit capitalism where it hurts, in its bottom line. The economy was already under stress because Europe and Japan, who had been devastated in WWII, were no longer in need of massive infrastructure investments but instead produced goods that competed with US output on the world market. National liberation threatened to push the prices of raw materials higher, later leading to the oil price shock of 1973 (profitable for the big oil companies but very costly for other businesses). At home, growing worker militancy, expressed in a rash of wildcat strikes, was raising wages and benefits while the new environmental movement was imposing new costs on industry. Even the effort to co-opt the Black power movement with the top-down "War on Poverty" entailed costs in terms of taxes.

To bring it all down to the bottom line, average profit rate for US business fell from a peak of 10% in 1965 to a low of 4.5% in 1974. And there was no way to simply swing out of this pit, which was only getting deeper. The healthy growth rates of the US economy from 1945 to 1970 were also cut in half for most of the ensuing decades and up through current times. The changes brought about have been sweeping. (The nature of this crisis and its impact on the prison industrial complex is discussed at book length in Christian Parenti's *Lockdown America*.)

The response on the international level has had two main features. Economically, the battering ram was the "Third World debt crisis." Big banks extended seemingly cheap loans to many of the poorest countries of what we now call the global South. Most of this money was wasted on lavish luxuries and military spending by US-supported dictators, doing nothing to develop those nations' economies. Then, the banks jacked the interest rates up so that these debts, even after payments totaling more than the original loans, just got bigger and bigger. The outstanding and unpayable debt became the basis for the IMF and WB to step in and impose "structural adjustment programs" (SAPs); about 70 of the world's poorest counties were under their thrall by the end of the 1980s. These SAPs imposed by international finance, including a set of austerity measures, were devastating for the people in those countries. The economic justification for this cruelty is "neoliberalism," which advocates radically reducing government help for the poor, opening up the country to foreign investment and goods, leaving social and economic decisions to the market. Of course this theory is a fraud, a pure rationalization by the dominant powers. Not one of today's developed countries got there in this way. All relied on tariffs to protect emerging industries and used considerable government guidance for national investment priorities. But neoliberalism has been a great success . . . in ratcheting down the costs of raw materials and manufactured components produced in the South for multinational corporations of the North.

At the same time, the major long-term political imperative has been to get the American public past its post-Vietnam reluctance to get involved in foreign wars. A series of presidents constructed a ladder of interventions, with various excuses, to take us from small, low-cost aggressions to bigger ones: from teeny Grenada in 1983, to small Panama in 1989, to medium-sized Iraq and then Serbia in the 1990s. All were designed to be quick and with minimal US casualties. A main method was to rely on intense aerial bombardments despite the horrendous toll of civilian casualties, which got whitewashed as "collateral damage." After quickly defeating Iraq's standing army in the 1991 Gulf War, the first President Bush couldn't help but exult, "We've kicked the Vietnam syndrome!" His celebration was a bit premature. But later the nightmare of 9/11/01 was seized by the rulers as a golden opportunity to exploit and channel Americans' fears into support for ever more ambitious foreign adventures.

Domestically a series of overlapping strategies have played out over this period. The Black struggle was the spearhead cracking open all kinds of potential for social change. So President Nixon, as his chief of staff H.R. Haldeman later recalled in his diary, "[…] emphasized that the whole problem is really the blacks. The key is to devise a system that recognizes this while not appearing to" (Quoted in Parenti). The government already had a secret and illegal campaign in play which resulted in the murders of scores of Black Panther, Native American, and other activists; the fostering of bitter internal splits within radical movements; and the tying up of thousands of organizers with bogus court cases and imprisonment. (For a book length account of just part of one of these programs, COINTELPRO, see Ward Churchill and Jim Vander Wall, *Agents of Repression*.)

The other level was against the community as a whole, under the rubric of "law and order." Whatever the government's level of complicity, the influx of drugs that took off at this time proved very destructive to unity and focus within the Black and Latin@ communities. Then the "War on Drugs" was even more devastating. There is no way this was a well-intentioned mistake. The US had already experienced Prohibition, which showed that outlawing a drug made the price skyrocket and thereby generated lethal violence and other crimes to build and control the trade. This misnamed war was conceived to mobilize the US public behind greatly increased police powers, used to cripple and contain the Black and Latin@ communities, and exploited to expand the state's repressive power with the proliferation of Police SWAT teams, the shredding of the 4th Amendment (against unreasonable search and seizure), and the burgeoning of the imprisoned population. And as we know, an even more intense level of police state measures were imposed in the wake of 9/11/01.

Even with political movements setback, the economy still stagnated in the 1970s. To boost profits, capital needed to cut labor costs at home. But a direct attack on wages and benefits at home was dangerous for the rulers, who relied on political support from large sectors of the predominantly white working class to be able to wage the foreign wars so essential to the system. In the post-civil rights US explicitly racist terms had to be avoided, but the drive shaft of internal politics became a railing against criminals, welfare mothers, and immigrants, which for most whites conjure up images of Blacks, Latin@s, and Asians, without being so impolite as to say that outright. To take just one small example of the dishonesty of these campaigns, the "tough on crime" politicians crusaded for cutbacks to both college classes and family visits for prisoners—the very two programs with the best proven success for reducing recidivism. Clearly the demagogs' concern wasn't to reduce crime to protect the good citizens but rather to redirect their frustrations toward those lower on the social ladder.

The sad irony is that many white working class people, such as the "Reagan Democrats," were organized in this way to build the political forces who then dismantled many of the 1930s gains for labor, as unions have been crippled and many of the better-paying jobs have been outsourced. White supremacy's companions-in-arms of patriarchy and class rule have also been enlisted in this forced march to the right. Women's independence has been undercut and the noxious flames of homophobia fanned with a hysterical "defense of the traditional family." Advocates for labor who try to hold back the rising flood waters of extreme inequality, the aggressive class warfare waged by the rich, are publicly denounced for "engaging in class warfare." All this hateful scapegoating doesn't simply divert people's view from the real, corporate sources of our problems, but also has served to consolidate the powers of the state to repress all forms of social advance.

## HIGHLY VOLATILE

Despite these sweeping changes and despite the severe setbacks to national liberation globally and to radical movements within the US, the struggle is far from over. Imperialism has not achieved anything like the stability and the sustained economic growth rates that followed WWII. The offensive to establish solid military control of the strategic Middle East is in disarray. Despite the false economic "truisms" of respectable opinion in the North, people throughout the South see through the lie of neoliberalism, and in South America especially there are promising mass mobilizations against it. At home, unease with the US imperial mission, worry about the economy, and concern about dangerous environmental damage have become widespread.

In response to the growing discontent, some elements within the establishment want to modify the current approach. This more enlightened sector would like less of the naked militarism and unilateralism that has badly hurt the US's image abroad. Domestically, they would like the skewed social priorities to be less extreme and less glaring. Some within the government have even raised cutting back on imprisoned populations to free some funds for such pressing needs as a health coverage system in shambles.

While such shifts may create some openings, I don't think we can expect much from these forces. For one thing they're still committed to the system, and imperialism cannot survive any major redistribution of wealth and power. Secondly, given that framework, the Right has had great success in shaping the debate by making certain topics totally taboo for public discussion. Let's look at two that are particularly relevant:

– Did US policies play a role in generating the hatreds that led to 9/11? Even mention of such a thought evokes a tsunami of vehement and discrediting vitriol. "Nothing can justify mass killings of civilians," is certainly true. But that's not at all a reason to avoid analyzing the causes of the event, something anyone sincerely concerned about protecting civilians would be eager to do, especially as Bush rages on with policies stoking the fires of violence and hatred. The very ones who scream "nothing justifies killing 3,000" simultaneously claim that those events, and even more the documented lies about them, justify the US's killing of tens of thousands of civilians. Rational discussion absolutely must be forbidden lest we get to the core reality of imperialism.

– Should we decriminalize drugs? When President Clinton's Surgeon General Jocelyn Elders simply suggested a study of decriminalization she was hooted off the public stage. In reality the "Drug War" has been a total failure in terms of stopping illegal drugs. Over the same 40 years, even the half-hearted public health campaign against the most addictive drug, tobacco, has cut the rate of smoking among adults in half. The public health alternative to the violence and destruction and billions of dollars of costs of the war is so obviously sound that it can't be considered lest it eliminate a campaign so essential to the politics of racial scapegoating and the mobilizing of public support for police powers.

In this upside-down world, radical alternatives, to the degree we can get them across to a large number of people, can make more sense than moderately chipping away at the dominant terms.

Imperialism has not fully regrouped, has not fully reconsolidated its rule from the turmoil and disruptions of 1968–73. Some of its very counter-offensives hold the potential for generating new shocks and crises. Bush's wars and policies in the Middle East seemed almost designed to ensure future attacks on Americans. The severity of environmental damage could set off more immediate disasters. Either of these problems could hurt an already shaky economy, where the gross inequality of wealth has cut into the level of consumption needed to keep it all going. The counter measure of pumping up the economy with massive infusions of debt entails the danger of making any contraction more dire, since consumers and businesses with debts to pay off won't be able to promptly put money back into consumption and production. I'm not saying that crises are necessarily imminent, the system can at times show great resilience, but the current situation is precarious.

## QUESTIONS FOR STRATEGY

We need to be wary of a common Left oversimplification that economic (or other) crises automatically provide fertile soil for organizing the workers against capitalism. The stark lesson of Nazi Germany, now echoed in the trends limned above, is that an imperialist power in crisis can resort to the most fulsome racial scapegoating as a way to mobilize the majority population for imperial reconquest abroad and for total repression of dissent at home. Crises can be dangerous; they are the only opportunities when we can build a visible, coherent, humane alternative. To do so we need to become a national movement powerful enough to shine a bright light on the corporate greed that is the real source of our problems; we need to grow to begin to embody the possibility of cooperation, from the bottom up, as the alternative to wars, recessions, environmental destruction, and a monstrous prison industrial complex.

The global South seethes with oppression and resistance, but does not yet have as well-defined and powerful a form of struggle as the national liberation struggles seemed to offer in the 60s and 70s. Within the US we probably now have a far greater number of people engaged in ongoing organizing projects, but without yet a sense of a strong national movement that can present an alternate vision and embody new hope. As the system enters deeper crisis, or alternatively limps along with giant unresolved problems, new space may open up for us as the old ways are discredited, but we also may face mounting dangers.

To me, if we hope to build an effective national movement we must directly challenge the attacks on immigrants, prisoners, and welfare recipients—not only as a matter of fundamental justice, but also because these arenas are crucial for blunting the strategic spearhead for right-wing mobilization. If we can confront those attacks and turn them around, we will take a big step toward setting new terms for political debate and change. The prison industrial complex constitutes a sobering aspect of the problem. Of course the PIC has nowhere near the economic size and political clout of its big brother, the military industrial complex. Nonetheless, now significant vested interests have been created who are all-too-ready to be a spark plug for the larger political engine of racial scapegoating.

At the same time, we don't have a chance of abolishing the PIC without opposing imperialism. The warfare and the security states go together and totally reinforce each other. We've seen this with a terrible vengeance in the post-9/11 world, where the isolation and torture of US prisons have been brought into play for a pivotal role in the "war on terror," which in turn has been used to ram through outrageous increases of police powers and denials of civil liberties, coming down hardest on the oppressed, but in place as a raised club threatening anyone who challenges the powers that be. If we don't challenge the larger system, the PIC remains on a solid foundation.

In short, we're likely to face a very challenging period ahead with great opportunities and dangers. Taking on the scapegoating of prisoners and others is essential to any success for the Left; an anti-imperialist framework and effort is crucial to any qualitative advance for prison industrial complex abolition.

In this situation there are a host of other questions for strategy. How can we bring a consciousness and liberatory politics about all the main pillars of the system—race, class, gender, and sexuality—into our daily work around specific issues? How can we transform ourselves around all these fundamentals while still pouring our energy into organizing and activism? How can we work from and advance a truly radical analysis and still reach out to large numbers of people? While there are as of yet no pat answers, CR organizers and others are doing invaluable work in consciously grappling with these and related issues in practice. I salute those frontline efforts. Let's all continue to move forward in a completely open-minded and full-hearted way.

DAVID GILBERT *has been a prisoner in New York State since 1981. A collection of his writings,* No Surrender, *is available from AK Press.*

**REFERENCES**

Ward Churchill and Jim Vander Wall, Agents of Repression (Boston: South End Press, 2002).
Christian Parenti, *Lockdown America: Police and Prisons in The Age of Crisis* (London: Verso, 1999).

# COPS AND THE VISUAL ECONOMY OF PUNISHMENT

*Ofelia Ortiz Cuevas*

In the middle of March 2002 I watched twenty-five young men, including my brother, attend a sentencing hearing in which eleven Mexican and/or Chicano, twelve African American, one white and one Asian men were sentenced cumulatively to 185 years behind bars. Leaving the courthouse, I saw a woman I recognized from the courtroom on her knees, crying loudly on the court house steps as people hurried by. She had just received news that her son—the brother of a young man who had just been sentenced to three years—had died earlier that morning in Pelican Bay state prison. That evening I came home to see "live" local news coverage of a low-speed car chase that ended with the two police dogs tearing at a young Black man's clothing as he laid on the ground somewhere in Los Angeles. Changing the channel, I saw more of the same—more car chases, more reality court hearings, more holding cells, more patrolling with *COPS*. That day it seemed like danger was everywhere. And for some it was.

This montage of scenes of power and punishment make up (for some) the dangerous terrain of life in California. Remarkable and yet part of the everyday, these scenes of punishment are everywhere. They have in a sense become significantly mundane. Imprisonment as a fix to social and economic crisis and the over-policing of working class and raced communities has grown at such a rate that it is difficult to miss scenes of state violence. As the US has increasingly come under the national and international scrutiny of civic and human rights organizations for the use of excessive and deadly force by police officers and for the horrifying numbers of humans caged, in what some prison scholars call the largest state project of the twentieth century, the visual economy of this reality has kept pace with the reality of mass imprisonment.

In New Jersey and New York alone, 150 people have been killed by police since September 11, 2001. Other instances in the last five years include the death of Gus Rugley, a 21-year-old Black man who was shot more than one hundred times by San Francisco police officers after a high speed chase; Cau Bich Tran, a 25-year-old Vietnamese woman shot by police in San Jose when they mistook her vegetable peeler for a gun; and Nathaniel Jones, beaten to death by metal baton after being taken into custody by Cincinnati police for shoplifting. While these incidents in particular were not visible to the general public, the visual display of racial punishment—of policing and state violence—are completely and continually visible in the realm of popular culture. Twenty-four hours a day, seven days a week, these scenes on the television or computer screen are accessible to be viewed in homes across the country. Spectacular car chases that end tragically with the death or brutal arrest of "suspected criminals" on local news channels, or the "real" life courtroom dramas shown on the endless disciplinary visual narrative of *Court TV*, the countless prison and crime documentaries that fill cable network stations such as A&E and the Discovery channel—these provide the viewing publics an increasingly closer look at the presumed reality of 21$^{st}$ century punishment.

Every evening on television, in news and dramatic programming, policed and punished Black and Brown bodies are part of the popular landscape of state-sanctioned domination and violence. So common and accepted, so significantly mundane is the brutality of the police against raced communities that the reality in which they are displayed before us become a social hallucination. The "racist disposition of the visible, which will prepare and achieve its own inverted perceptions under the rubric of *what is seen*," according to Judith Butler can turn a clear vision of police brutality into a myth of "police vulnerability." Thus the violence enacted upon Rodney King, who was clearly beaten by police, becomes not a case of state brutality but a reality so twisted that it is seen as a case of police victimization. The violence of policing is so common and accepted that even as death lingers in local news footage of the bullet-ridden car where 13-year-old Devon Brown was repeatedly shot to death by the Los Angeles Police Department (LAPD) in 2005 for joyriding, the scene becomes at best another "heart-breaking tragedy" and at worst simply another image in the visual regime of racial punishment that fills the television airwaves. We no longer stand as witnesses to brutality, we gather in front of televisions (and computer screens) as publics entertained by racial punishment. The regimes of visuality, those institutions that mobilize our vision, twist the meaning of humanity such that violence and death for some become pleasure for others.

Marking two decades of the inside reality of policing, the creators and producers of *COPS* are releasing a special DVD edition for the program's 20th anniversary, making *COPS* one of the longest running shows in television history. *COPS* has provided a relentless display of chased, cuffed, tackled, tazered, choked, stomped, berated, humiliated, stripped, bloodied, and shot Black, Brown, and poor bodies. The show commonly displays images of men in chokeholds with several police officers twisting their limbs as they scream in pain or men and women pinned on the ground with shotgun and rifles pointed at the backs of their head or families crying as children are torn from their mother's arms by state officials. The newest edition to punishment as entertainment, *JAIL*—also produced by John Langley, the creator of *COPS*—displays the spectacle that follows "processing" people who are arrested. The program focuses on holding cells filled with screaming suspects, the forced fingerprinting and photographing of suspects, and displays men and women deemed too dangerous for general population restrained on gurneys. So successful have these scenes of punishment been—the compelling images of humiliation and human debasement—that reality crime programming has gone global. The brutality of state violence can now be seen on *Placas* in Mexico City, *The Force* in Australia, *Nyom nélkül* in Hungary, and *Police Camera Action* in the UK. And although Langley has claimed the show unprecedented in its view of the raw reality of policing the bad guys—these spectacular displays of punishment do have precedents.

These spectacles of punishment and torture are not new so much as they are resurrected and rearticulated forms of past brutalities in which crowds gathered to watch in the name of "justice." The visual presentation of punished bodies has played a continuous role in the political and economic projects of the US—projects dangerous to the populations that threatened or resisted the ideals and progress of capital. Racial punishment displayed for entertainment and popular consumption has long been common. The photo documentation of the massacre at Wounded Knee, the early mug shots documenting Chinese "delinquency" in California, the head of Joaquin Murrieta on tour in California bars and saloons, the World War Two-era newspaper coverage of the Japanese interned, or of Zoot-suiters disrobed on the streets of Los Angeles—all are images of racial punishment situated within terrains of crisis and accumulation.

During the Reconstruction period and into the early 1900s, a dramatic and volatile shift in the imprisonment of Blacks also addressed the terrain of crisis. In that era and into the turn of the twentieth century, the dramatic growth in individuals relegated to the punishment system was so vast that W.E.B Du Bois was moved to exclaim that, "In no other part of the modern world has there been so open and conscious a traffic in crime for deliberate social degradation and private profit as in the South." Du Bois was acknowledging the systematic rearticulation of slavery upon which the rebuilding of the South depended, and which existed under the guise of a legitimate "criminal justice system." He was in part referring to the laws which regulated slavery and were immediately re-addressed to manage the crisis brought on by the newly-freed population of Blacks in the South. This reanimated labor, which first took the form of the convict lease system and later of the chain gang, could be seen by the 1900s in the long rows of men chained to one another along railroad lines or new public roads. Working long hours under threat of the "whipping boss," the convicts—visible signifiers of reestablished order—were evidence of the institutionalization of brutality which was part of the reason for the existence of the convict lease system. Violence, according to Matthew Mancini, was not grafted onto a particular system of penal management—the system of convict lease was maintained as an institutional outlet for violence.

During this same period, the violence enacted against the Black body had reached an apex of spectacular punishment which Ida B. Wells documented in her work on lynching in the US. In *Red Record: Mob Rule in New Orleans*, Wells detailed the executions of Blacks by public mobs as part of her campaign against lynching. Wells described the violent public deaths of Calvin Thomas in Georgia, who was accused of assault; Charles T. Miller in Kentucky for alleged rape; Isaac Lincoln in South Carolina for insulting a white person; Andy Blount for suspicion of rape in Tennessee; and an "Unknown Negro" for self-defense in Kentucky. Her list of lynching victims included detailed descriptions of the mob and the activities of the spectators who attended, as she stated, "in crowds of thousands, from cities all over the South with some who watched calmly while others cheered and clapped." Wells accounted for the men, women, and children who were caught up in the frenzy of the event and took away body parts, fingers, hair, and the charred remains of the people burned, as well as pieces of the hangman's noose. She explained that the teeth, hair and fingers of Lee Walker, in Georgia, were taken from his burned body; Wells described an "Unknown Negro" also in Georgia who was run down, dragged through town by a rope, hung and left for townspeople to shoot. Quoting an eyewitness to the burning of Henry Smith (a Black man charged with the murder of a four-year-old white girl), Wells wrote, "Even at the stake, children of both sexes and colors gathered in groups ... The children became as frantic as the grown people ... Little faces distorted with passion and the bloodshot eyes of the cruel parent watched with glee the burning body of Smith." According to Wells, ten thousand people watched the hanging and burning of Henry Smith. His body became the focal point for the anxiety, fear, desire, and loathing of white Americans.

The point of resurrecting this history is not to argue that prisons or policing are literally equivalent to lynching, but to suggest that the contemporary era of prison-building and policing is part of a racial punishment regime that shares a genealogy with the institution of slavery, and the brutal acquisition of Mexican and Indian land—all are ways in which violence is used against the racial body in a time of crisis. Resurrecting this past is to recognize in the present a "moment of danger." In Walter Benjamin's transfixing contemplation of history, he compels us to be aware of the past: the past carries with it a temporal index by which it is referred to redemption. There is a secret agreement between past generations and the present one. For Benjamin, the past is not being rearticulated and presented "as it really was," he states, but should be seized in a moment of danger, which he understands as that instant "when an image flashes up."

This moment of danger became a moment of opportunity in the year 2000. While the US made history as the largest jailer on the planet, a photo art book titled *Without Sanctuary: Lynching Photography in the United States* was published. The book was based on a museum exhibition of postcard photographs of lynching. Both the exhibition and book revealed in gruesome detail practices from apex of racial discipline which lasted from the later half of the 1800s until the 1960s. The public was shocked, for a moment at least, at the level of violence and brutality. The extreme nature of lynching practices and the participation of modern audiences revealed a disjuncture in the understanding the US has of itself as a country that had presumably overcome (or purposely forgotten) this dark history. *Without Sanctuary*'s reception indexed the forced historical and racial amnesia necessary to the forgetting and refashioning of a now-incomprehensible brutal and uncivilized practice of racial discipline. The tortured and terrorized bodies of those who transgressed social norms and threatened the material value of white accumulation were seen as victims of inconceivable acts of hate and human evil that have long since been overcome by humanitarian progress. This moment came and went. The possibility that such brutal forms of racial punishment had not entirely died away was only manifested with references to the "modern day lynchings" of the clandestine brutal murders of James Byrd and Amadou Diallo. Missed in this too-literal translation is the sanctioned violent disciplinary practices of the police state in the 21$^{st}$ century, those acts of violence and brutality against the racial body seen everyday on television.

Although the precise mechanisms through which the criminalized Black and Brown body is targeted, displayed, and then visually consumed have changed drastically over the past eighty years, the practice of public punishment and its ramifications remain remarkably similar. The shot, maimed, debased, and dehumanized subjected bodies seen from the comfort of home on *COPS* and the 2.5 million imprisoned are the unrecognized subjects of this moment eclipsed by the negotiation of "reality" presented in the pages of *Without Sanctuary*. Very few viewers of *Without Sanctuary* were able to see their own society reflected in the images of lynching hanging on the museum walls or in the glossy pages of the photo art book.

The public enlisted by *COPS* (and other realisms of punishment) gathers in front of television sets across the country to watch the capture, discipline, and containment of "bad" subjects/suspects. Because *COPS* is presented in a "reality" format it functions as a cultural axis upon which the visuality of race, class, and punishment are formed. Similarly, the postcards of lynched bodies in *Without Sanctuary* powerfully highlight the connection between 19th century racial violence and the naturalization of a racial order. Their exhibition and publication encouraged their audience to rethink the relationship between the racial body and public punishment in the 20th and 21st century. Although the precise mechanisms through which the criminalized body of color is targeted, displayed, and visually consumed have changed drastically over the past eighty years, the practice of public punishment and its ramifications remain remarkably similar.

The images of reality policing and imprisonment are situated in ways that allow race and class to be consumed with a certain consensual understanding and a moral indignation that works to naturalize the discriminatory reality of state structures. That is, answering the hail of the state, the citizen-witness comes to comply with common sense notions of what is legitimately watchable and believable and what is sanctionable. On *COPS* and in the images of *Without Sanctuary*, the crime is presumed to be self evident, embedded in the social consciousness as a point of departure. The public that is summoned to watch and be entertained is already in compliance with the legitimacy and rectitude of the punishment of the racial body. Even when there is relatively little actual bloodshed, these scenes of racial discipline are typically permeated by the power of the state, by its violence, coercion and repression, and by the concrete embodiment of abstract social forces mutually constituted by the visual regimes that emerge from the realm of popular culture itself. Through the regimes of visuality, the body on *COPS* and in *Without Sanctuary* exists as an ideological offering that sutures the contradiction between the ideals of democracy and the reality of massive police repression and imprisonment in a time of empire building and globalization.

The logic of terror and violence enacted upon the Black and Brown bodies that are identified in the present as "criminal" is reliant on inverted perceptions—in this case where brutal assailants become the victims or heroes. These visions of racial punishment are twisted into social hallucinations that legitimize policing and imprisonment. These twisted or inverted perceptions emerge from a whole constellation of institutional structures situated within histories where the meaning and the value of the racial body is actualized in the moment of its destruction at the hand of the state. Structures such as the courtroom, or the police car, or the booking station force a perception of justice marked by institutional symbols seen within a field of vision of reality: the police uniform and badge, the judge's robe, the sanctioned gun. Despite this, they are hallucinations of justice.

OFELIA ORTIZ CUEVAS *is a U.C. President's Postdoctoral Fellow in the Department of Ethnic Studies at University of California, Riverside. Her research focuses on visual regimes of punishment, the racial body, crisis, and the state.*

# AUTOBIOGRAPHY @ 33

*Eddy Zheng*

I am 33 years old and breathin'
it's a good year to die
to myself
I never felt such extreme peace
despite being mired in constant ear-deafening screams
from the caged occupants – triple CMS*, PCs**, gang validated,
    drop-outs, parole violators, lifers,
    drug casualties, three strikers,
    human beings
    in San Quentin's 150 year old solitary confinement
    I don't want to start things over
    @ 33
I am very proud of being who I am
I wrote a letter to a stranger who said
    "You deserve to lose at least your youth,
        not returning to society until well into middle age … "
after reading an article about me in *San Francisco Weekly*
I told him
    "A hundred years from now when we no
    longer exist on this earth of humankind the
    seriousness of my crime will not be changed
    or lessened. I can never pay my debt to the

victims because I cannot turn back the hands
of time ... I will not judge you."
whenever I think about my crime I feel ashamed
I've lost my youth and more
I've learned that the more I suffer the stronger I become
I am blessed with great friends
I talk better than I write
because the police can't hear my conversation
the prison officials labeled me a trouble maker
I dared to challenge the administration for its civil rights violation
I fought for Ethnic Studies in the prison college program
I've been a slave for 16 years under the 13th Amendment
I know separation and disappointment intimately
I memorized the United Front Points of Unity
I love my family and friends
my shero Yuri Kochiyama and a young sister named Monica
who is pretty wanted to come visit me
somehow I have more female friends than male friends
I never made love to a woman
sometimes I feel like 16
but my body disagrees
some people called me a square
because I don't drink, smoke, or do drugs
I am a procrastinator but I get things done
I've never been back to my motherland
I started to learn Spanish
escribió una poema en español
at times I can be very selfish and vice versa
I've never been to a prom, concert, opera, sporting event
or my parents' house
I don't remember the last time I cried
I've sweat with the Native Americans, attended mass with the
Catholics, went to service with the Protestants, sat and chanted
with the Buddhists
my mind is my church
I am spoiled
in 2001 a young lady I love stopped loving me
it felt worse than losing my freedom

I was denied parole for the ninth time
I assured Mom that I will be home one day
after she pleaded me to answer her question truthfully
    "Are you ever going to get out of prison?"
the Prison Industrial Complex and its masters attempted to
control my mind
    it didn't work
they didn't know I've been introduced to Che, Yuri Kochiyama,
Paulo Freire, Howard Zinn, Frederick Douglass, Assata Shakur, bell hooks
Maurice Cornforth, Malcolm X, Gandhi, Geroge Jackson, Mumia, Budda
and many others ...
I had about a hundred books in my cell
I was internalizing my politics
In 2000 I organized the first poetry slam in San Quentin
I earned my associate of art degree
something that I never thought possible
I've self-published a zine
I was the poster boy for San Quentin
some time in the '90s my grandparents died
without knowing that I was in prison
@ 30
I kissed Dad on the cheek and told him that I love him for the first time
I've written my first poem
I called myself a poet to motivate me to write
because I knew poets would set us free
in 1998 I was granted parole
                      then it was taken away
the governor's political career superceded my life
some time in the 90s I participated in most of the self help program
in 1996 I really learned how to read and write
I read my first history book "A People's History of the United States"
my social conscious mind was awakened
in 1992 I pass my GED in Solano Prison
I learned how to take care of my body from '89 to '93
in 1987 I turned 18 and went to the Pen from youth authority
the youngest prisoner in San Quentin's Maximum Security Prison
I was lucky people thought I knew kung fu
@ 16

I violated an innocent family of four and scarred them for life
money superceded human suffering
I was charged as an adult and sentenced to life with a possibility
no hablo ingles
I wish I could start things over
I was completely lost
@ 12
I left Communist China to Capitalist America
no hablo ingles
I was spoiled
in 1976 I went to demonstrations against the Gang of Four
life was a blur from 1 to 6
on 5/29/69
I inhaled my first breath

*Correctional Clinical Case Management System
    Mental health condition of prisoners
**Protective Custody of Prisoners

**EDDY ZHENG** *works for the Community Youth center in San Francisco as a Project Coordinator for the Community Response Network—Asian Pacific Islanders. He is an advisory board member of the Asian American Law Journal. Eddy is the recipient of the Bay Area Asian Pacific American Law Students Association's Outstanding Leadership Award for 2008 and Chinese World Journal newspaper's Community Hero Award of 2007. Eddy led a book project which culminated in the publication of* Other: An Asian and Pacific Islander Prisoners' Anthology. *Eddy accomplished these after he spent 21 years in prison for crimes he committed at the age of 16. For more information please go to www.eddyzheng.com, www.myspace.com/asianprisoners, or www.eddyzheng.blogspot.com*

*Reprinted from* Other: an Asian & Pacific Islander Prisoners' Anthology, *with permission from the Asian Prisoner Support Committee (APSC).* Other *is the first book to highlight the unique stories and perspectives of the growing Asian prisoner population in the US. It is available now on Amazon.com.*

# BLACK BURDEN
*Jimi Marshall*

What is it to be the Black Burden?

To be viewed by the world as a liability, not asset? To be forced to experience life through cast-down eyes and longing glares.

Never allowed to stand firm or proud even in ones own home. What exactly am I to be proud of? Am I to be proud of the fact that P-Diddy has acquired the latest colored mink coat while millions of my Brothers and Sisters perish from starvation and continue to be denied their basic human rights? What is it to realize that every money-hungry merchant first to have my commodities' dollars detest doing business with the people of that community. What is it to know that when I step to the table of the World Commerce I come empty handed and Nationless even though I am responsible for the construction of numerous empires.

What is it to realize that when the world pictures a thief, murderer or rapist it is in my image. When the topic of AIDS enters a conversation it comes dressed in my skin. When the so-called music of today is glorified as hip, in reality is nothing more than a rally cry for my destruction and a testament of my self-hatred.

What is it to know the course of action yet fear to take it. That is the Black Burden. A burden which lies heavy on my very own conscience.

4-27-05

JIMI MARSHALL *is a thirty-seven-year-old man of African descent, who is serving a life sentence for first degree murder. He has been imprisoned since he was seventeen, and is currently in Correctional Training Facility in Soledad, CA. He is from the Long Beach area.*

# SECTION 2:
# CHANGE

# NO ONE IS CRIMINAL

*Martha Escobar*

Attending almost any immigrant rights event, especially the marches of the last three years, or conducting an online image search of the words "immigrant rights march" exposes the predominant message immigrant rights advocates attempt to convey—"immigrants are not criminals, immigrants are hard workers." Similarly, the now iconic message "Nadie es Ilegal/No One is Illegal" invariably appears during marches and protests and on banners, t-shirts, pins, and so forth. These messages that attempt to distance immigrants from criminality are prevalent and central to the mainstream immigrant rights movement because they try to secure the innocence and safety of communities that are constantly under intense policing and violence. However, these decriminalizing motions turn into violent acts themselves when the innocence of some is secured at the expense of "others." The identity of immigrant and the identity of criminal become mutually exclusive, largely constructing immigrants as innocent while criminalizing unspoken "others." When the innocence of immigrants is articulated, we are left to ask "If immigrants are not the criminals, then who are? If immigrants are innocent, then who is guilty?" In what follows I provide a discussion of the development of the notion of "criminal" in the US, highlighting some of the ways that the concept is constructed primarily around Blackness and Black bodies. Thus when we claim that immigrants are not criminals, the fundamental message is that immigrants are not Black, or at least, that immigrants will not be "another Black problem." Tracing the construction of criminality in relationship to Blackness and how it is re-mapped onto brown bodies through the notion of "illegality" gives witness to the ways that criminality allows a reconfiguration of racial boundaries along Blackness and whiteness. In other words, criminalizing immigrants serves to discipline them into whiteness.

This essay is largely informed by critical anthropologist, Nicholas De Genova and his work, *Working the Boundaries: Race, Space, and "Illegality" in Mexican Chicago*. Through this project he examines how "Mexican migrants in Chicago negotiated their own re-racialization as Mexican, always in relation to both a dominant whiteness and its polar opposite, a subjugated and denigrated Blackness" (8). De Genova illustrates how the anti-immigrant politics of the 1990s were inherently tied to the criminalization and dismantling of social welfare for impoverished US citizens, largely imagined as Black. What results is what he calls double discipline (206). On the one side, migrants are made responsible for "taking American jobs," on the other, their vulnerability as migrant workers encourages them to generate distance between themselves and impoverished US citizens constructed as "lazy" and racialized as Black. Claiming the identity of "hard workers" led to disparaging the "laziness" of impoverished citizens who had advantages over migrants, such as the knowledge of the English language and citizenship (206). According to De Genova, "Because migrant workers were always at pains to demonstrate to their overseers that they were 'hardworking' and not 'lazy,' the momentum of their efforts at self-defense served to subvert the possibilities for resistance, and they effectively participated in their own intensified exploitation" (206, cites Kearny 1996: 156; 1998: 29).

The white supremacist social order of the US fixed Mexican migrants spatially between whites and Blacks. However, their own "illegal" transnationality permanently dislodged them from "American"-ness. Furthermore, it is crucial to note how criminality is feminized. Criminality historically is conceptualized as being birthed by Black women, so how does this inform the criminalization of immigrants? The merging of criminality and state dependency does not only result in attempts to distance immigrants from Blackness, but the feminization of criminality also results in immigrant rights activists grasping on to masculinized claims of immigrants as hard workers. Through the examination of immigrant rights discourse that attempts to denaturalize immigrant criminality and fasten the identity of migrant to "hard worker," I do not only reinforce De Genova's position that migrants' negotiation between the polarized racial boundaries of the US often results in bolstering white supremacy, but also mark it as a particularly violent patriarchal negotiation.

Several authors have traced the historical development of criminality around Black bodies. In *Are Prisons Obsolete?*, prison abolitionist Angela Y. Davis provides this analysis from the post-reconstruction era to the present. She examines the ways that the Thirteenth Amendment of the US Constitution served to re-enslave recently freed Black slaves by constructing Blacks as criminal. The amendment states: "Neither slavery nor involuntary servitude, *except as a punishment for crime* whereof the party shall have been duly convicted, shall exist within the United States, or any place subject to their jurisdiction." Davis shows how passing Black Codes, legislation enacted to criminalize the behavior of Blacks, including vagrancy, unemployment, and missing work, changed prison demographics from predominantly white to largely Black prisoners (28).

The South produced the convict leasing system which provided Black bodies that were "leased" to meet the labor needs generated with the abolition of slavery and developing industrial capitalism.[1] Davis continues and argues that a similar relationship exists between the contemporary Black imprisonment and profitability (68). While prisoners' labor continues to yield some economic revenue, the major profiteering occurs through industries that service prisons to meet the needs of over two million people in prison, such as food, clothing, health care, and so forth.[2] Over half of the prison population is comprised of Black men, underscoring how Black male bodies continue to be made expendable, and criminality continues to serve as the marker of difference that constructs their disposability.[3]

However, there is a particular conceptualization of crisis-informed Black criminality that develops during the 1960s. Christian Parenti examines the social movements of the 60s and 70s and convincingly argues that the United States was in a state of crisis produced by the social upheavals of the time, particularly the militancy of groups such as the Black Panthers. Parenti writes, "America's whole social fabric seemed to be coming apart. Every structure of authority and obedience was breaking down. Though garnished with youthful nudity and flowers, the crisis of the late sixties and early seventies was more serious than is often acknowledged; the country was in the midst of a haphazard but deadly social revolution" (4).

---

1   Alex Lichtenstein makes a similar argument in, *"Except as a Punishment for Crime," Twice the Work of Free Labor: The Political Economy of Convict Labor in the New South*, p. 17–36. He maintains that unlike slavery, which necessitated the maintenance of slaves by slave masters, the convict leasing system was worse because not only did slaves have to work, but they were dispensable; there was an endless supply of Black bodies for labor.

2   Key works that center the profitability of prisons include Katherine Beckett, *Making Crime Pay: Law and Order in Contemporary American Politics*, New York: Oxford University Press, 1997; Daniel Burton-Rose, Dan Pens, and Paul Wright, *The Celling of America: An Inside Look at the US Prison Industry*, Monroe, ME: Common Courage Press, 1998; Joel Dyer, *The Perpetual Prisoner Machine: How America Profits from Crime*, Boulder: Westview Press, 1999.

3   Jerome Miller discusses this in his book *Search and Destroy: African-American Males in the Criminal Justice System*. Central works that discuss the criminalization and imprisonment of Blacks include Marc Mauer, *Race to Incarcerate*, New York: The New Press, 1999; and Michel Tonry, *Malign Neglect: Race, Crime and Punishment in America*, New York: Oxford University Press, 1995.

According to Parenti, national security shifts from focusing on foreign threats to security from domestic violence. He locates this shift in Barry Goldwater's 1964 Republican presidential nomination acceptance speech: "Security from domestic violence, no less than from foreign aggression is the most elementary form and fundamental purpose of any government." Goldwater promised that "enforcing law and order" would be central to his presidency. Although Goldwater lost to Johnson, his rhetoric won out. A new form of politics was instituted: the domestic war on bodies racialized as non-white, particularly Blacks. Richard Nixon followed in Johnson's steps as the following excerpt from a letter addressed to Dwight Eisenhower demonstrates: "I have found great audience response to this [law-and-order] in all parts of the country, including areas like New Hampshire where there is virtually no race problem and relatively little crime." The constructed crisis—the loss of "law and order"—unites crime to urban and urban to Blackness (7). The policies that develop to contain the "crime" crisis are thus policies constructed to control Black bodies.

The production of Black lawlessness and disorder merged with changes occurring to the welfare state. During this time the doors of the welfare system were forced open to allow previously excluded people access, increasing enrollment from 2 million people to 13 million. This included African Americans, divorced, separated, deserted, and increasingly never-married women—people determined as the "undeserving poor." These changes directed the public's anxiety towards single-Black mothers, children born to single mothers, and generational dependency in the program.[4] Single, poor, particularly Black mothers were believed to be morally *different* from "deserving mothers" who were either dependent on their husbands or self-sufficient.[5] Welfare policy and welfare administration has historically served to pass moral judgment on who is deserving and who is undeserving.

Historian Michael B. Katz discusses the construction of the "undeserving poor" through the discourse of personal choice. In other words, poverty is self-made by the poor choices that those in poverty make, constructing poor people as undeserving. He writes, "They remained different and inferior because, whatever their origins, the actions and attitudes of poor people themselves assured their continued poverty and that of their children" (16). By the 1980s there was alarm and hostility towards people in poverty: "What bothered observers most was not their suffering; rather, it

4    Mimi Abramowitz, *Regulating the Lives of Women: Social Welfare Policy from Colonial Times to the Present*, Boston: South End Press, 1988.

5    Joel Handler, "Welfare Reform: Tightening the Screws," in *Women at the Margins: Neglect, Punishment, and Resistance*, edited by Josefina Figueira-McDonough and Rosemary C. Sarri, New York: The Hawthorn Press, 2002: 34.

was their sexuality, expressed in teenage pregnancy; family patterns, represented by female-headed households; alleged reluctance to work for low wages; welfare dependence, incorrectly believed to be a major drain on national resources; and propensity for drug use and violent crime, which had eroded the safety of the streets and the subways" (185). Through the rhetoric of personal responsibility, families with single Black mothers were held responsible for social problems like low levels of education, teen pregnancy, and poverty, all of which coalesced in the national imagination as leading to increased crime.[6] Feminist scholar Dorothy Roberts writes that "Society penalizes Black single mothers not only because they depart from the norm of marriage as prerequisite to pregnancy but also because they represent rebellious Black culture."[7] Considering Parenti's argument that Black rebelliousness was made criminal through the language of "law and order," Black women's reproduction was thus responsible for "breeding" this imagined crisis. According to Patricia Hill Collins, not only were welfare recipients, largely conceptualized as Black women, rendered unfit to pass on national culture, but punitive practices against this group, including curtailing their reproduction, were legitimized.[8]

Whereas "working-class Black women are constructed as the enemy within, the group producing the population that threatens the American national interest of maintaining itself as a 'White' nation-state" (126), immigrant women are constructed as the enemy coming from the outside, crossing the border "illegally" to have children. Concerns in California over dependent immigrant women were developed by making use of already existing images of the "welfare queen." Employing the same discourse on immigrant women as was used to criminalize Black motherhood disciplines them into ideal citizen behavior, particularly discouraging access to state resources. During the 1990s the unworthiness of immigrants, voiced within the language of public charge produced around Black motherhood, carried over the connotation of "criminal," an identity crystallized by their assumed "illegal" entrance into the US, rendering immigrant brown bodies as perpetual criminals.

Mapping criminality onto brown bodies occurs in large part through the notion of "immigrant illegality." The criminalization of immigrants is secured through

---

6    Ronald Reagan made the image of the "welfare queen" everlasting when in 1976 he gave a presidential campaign speech and cited alleged news stories, "She has 80 names, 30 addresses, 12 Social Security cards and is collecting veteran's benefits on four non-existing deceased husbands. And she is collecting Social Security on her cards. She's got Medicaid, getting food stamps, and she is collecting welfare under each of her names." Although the story was later discredited, the message lived on.

7    Roberts cites Austin 1989: 557 and Solinger 1992a: 25(238).

8    Hill Collins, 1999: 126.

their assumed "illegal" entrance into the US. Images of Mexican migrants "flooding" the US-Mexico border saturate the media, constructing a crisis of "invasion". As is the case in Black people's criminalization, women's reproduction is also targeted. Migrant women are imagined as crossing the border "illegally" to secure not only their children's citizenship, but their own eventually, and undeservingly, accessing resources such as health care and education. The merging of criminality and state dependency is evident in several state policies passed in the past few decades. An examination of some of these policies reveals how the notions of "public charges" and "criminals," racialized ideas that are historically formed around Black bodies, are mapped on to brown bodies.

Consider the introduction to California's Proposition 187, "Save Our State" (S.O.S.):

> The people of California find and declare as follows: That they have suffered and are suffering economic hardship caused by the presence of illegal aliens in the state. That they have suffered and are suffering personal injury and damage caused by the criminal conduct of illegal aliens in this state. That they have suffered and are suffering personal injury and damage caused by the criminal conduct of illegal aliens in the state. That they have a right to the protection of their government from any person or persons entering this country unlawfully.[9]

Californians are discursively constructed as victims of "illegal aliens" and their inherent criminality, and declare a right to "protection" from this enemy. The proposals made by the policy required local and state agencies to report undocumented applicants, in addition to prohibiting undocumented people from accessing publicly funded social services, education, welfare, and non-emergency health.[10] In short, the proposition targeted women's reproduction and their children, and framed immigrants as enemy criminals. Proposition 187 effectively re-fused state dependency and criminality and made migrant women and their children the enemy to be protected from.

Although Proposition 187 was declared unconstitutional, in 1996 Bill Clinton signed into effect the Personal Responsibility and Work Opportunity Act (Welfare Reform Act) which implemented many of the proposals made through Proposition 187. For example, it barred state and local governments from providing all but emergency services to undocumented people, prohibited documented immigrants,

---

9    1994 California Voter Information: Proposition 187. Text of proposed Law.

10    Kent A. Ono and John M. Sloop, *Shifting Borders: Rhetoric, Immigration, and California's Proposition 187*, Philadelphia: Temple University Press, 2002: 3.

unwed teen mothers, and children born to mothers already on welfare from receiving public benefits, and denied assistance and benefits for people with drug-related convictions. Evident in the Welfare Reform Act is the merging of state dependency, criminality, and immigration. Sociologist Lisa Sun-Hee Park provides an analysis of the notion of "public charge" in conjunction with the 1996 Welfare Reform and argues that "the social contexts that helped garner support for such anti-immigrant legislative measures created an environment that essentially criminalized motherhood for low-income immigrant women—whether they are documented or undocumented" (1161). Migrant women's criminalization is multifaceted, but two large contributing factors are their "illegal" border-crossing, automatically criminalizing them, and their imagined reproduction of future "criminals."

Merging criminality and dependency around immigrant bodies is also evidenced through the enactment of the Illegal Immigration Reform and Immigrant Responsibility Act of 1996 (IIRIRA), intended to decrease the number of undocumented immigrants in the US. IIRIRA passed one month after the Welfare Reform Act and reinforced restrictions on immigrant welfare use. Furthermore, it expanded the state's ability to deport non-citizens with criminal records, resulting in an exponential expansion in the deportation of non-citizens. In 1986, for example, there was a removal of 1,978 immigrants for criminal violations. In 2004, the number increased to 82,802, a 41.86% increase.[11]

The immigration debate occupies an extremely important position in the national imagination. The debate is predominantly structured within binary constructions and the immigrant rights movement is limited to this framework.[12] When immigrants are called drains on the economy, rebuttals to this statement include that immigrants take the jobs that others do not want, they use less resources than non-immigrants, and are unable to collect income taxes resulting in unclaimed funds. When arguments are made that immigrants are changing the national culture, re-

---

11    US Immigration and Customs Enforcement, "ICE Removes Career Criminal," *Inside ICE*, Volume 2, No. 6, March 14, 2005: 5. Accessed 7/24/08. http://www.ice.gov/doclib/pi/news/insideice/articles/InsideICE031405.pdf

12    Leland Saito (1998) examines the binaries of "good" immigrants and "bad" immigrants and highlights how these binary ideas help in the erasure of the historical oppression of people racialized as non-white. "Good immigrants" are described as people who "try to 'blend in and adapt to the ways of America.' That is, they should be passive and subservient. They certainly should not challenge the economic and political order of their newly adopted city" (341). Saito notes that "Implicit in this complaint is the assimilation perspective, which assumes that complete acceptance into the mainstream is possible, ignoring the history of exclusion experienced by Asian Americans, Latinos, and African Americans" (341).

sponses include citing bilingualism and biculturalism as positive developments that benefit the United States. We are fixed in a polarized debate that does little to arrive at the root causes of migration and the role the US has in creating and maintaining it. The criminality component of the debate differs little from this pattern. When immigrants are represented as criminals, the reaction is to distance immigrants from criminality and move them closer to "American"-ness by stating that immigrants are not criminals, immigrants are hard workers. However, this effort is framed within the context of a criminality that is mutually exclusive from the national "American" identity that is wedded to whiteness. Thus, immigrant Americanizing efforts are negotiations between racial whiteness and racial Blackness.

Criminologists Ramiro Martinez Jr. and Abel Valenzuela Jr. recently edited and published *Immigration and Crime: Race, Ethnicity, and Violence*, a project dedicated to challenging stereotypes of immigrant criminality.[13] Martinez and Valenzuela maintain that contrary to popular belief, the increased presence of immigrants does not affect and, in some cases, actually reduces levels of crime and violence (10; 13). The vast majority of the book is dedicated to locating and assessing immigrant criminality without engaging in the discussion of criminalization.[14] In other words, this project naturalizes crime as a fact and argues for the innocence of immigrants. Several of the authors cite that involvement in crime changes across generations, presumably as they acculturate.[15] In other words, the longer the family's stay in the US, the higher the likelihood of engaging in crime.

One example that links criminality to acculturation is Min Zhou and Carl L. Bankston's "Delinquency and Acculturation in the Twenty-first Century." In this piece the authors examine "an apparent increase in problem behavior among Vietnamese young people" (117). They cite an earlier study where they found that living in tight ethnic communities provided some control over Vietnamese youth. Zhou and Bankston argued that these ethnic enclaves allowed for the dissemination of cultural values, such as respect, obedience, and hard work, resulting in school success (120). However, also present in these enclaves were marginalized Vietnamese youth who, according to the authors, "were simply disoriented drifters and school dropouts, while others were lawless gangsters. Many of these alienated youth had families characterized by absent parents, poor relations among family members,

---

13   New York: New York University Press, 2006.

14   The exception is Sang Hea Kil and Cecilia Menjívar's article, "'The 'War on the Border': Criminalizing Immigrants and Militarizing the U.S.-Mexico Border," 164–188. Rather than attempting to locate immigrant criminality, Kil and Menjívar center state policies, including the militarization of the border, and link these practices to the increased public violent response against immigrants.

15   Some examples include Morenoff and Astor, Rumbaut et al., and Zhou and Bankston.

weak connections to other Vietnamese families, or a lack of involvement in the Vietnamese community" (120). The authors considered these families problematic because of their detachment from their community. Ten years after their first study Zhou and Bankston reconsider the same question with a new generation. What changed after ten years? According to the authors, there is an increased possibility that Vietnamese youth are acculturating, moving away from their ethnic ties and towards increased delinquency (137). They argue that "a general trend has become clear: more and more adolescents are moving closer to the subculture of their American peers and away from their Vietnamese community. However, those in the nondelinquent cluster tended to report having more white friends than those in the delinquent cluster" (130). Although Zhou and Bankston provide caveats and maintain that it is unfair to infer that the more that Vietnamese youth associate with Blacks the more they will engage in delinquency, their conclusions reinforce this idea. The authors maintain that successful integration into the larger society depends on the fit between familial and ethnic social systems on the one hand and on the fit between the ethnic social systems and the larger society on the other. The local social environment, including both American and Americanized peer groups, pulls young people into the ethnic community and the more the ethnic community guides them towards normative orientations consistent with those of the larger society, the less those young people are drawn towards the alternative social circles of local youth (136).

Who are the local youth? According to the authors' study, Vietnamese communities, including those they base their study on, are located in predominantly Black neighborhoods. Thus, the local youth that Zhou and Bankston cite as drawing Vietnamese youth away from their communities and towards delinquency are Black youth. The authors' attempt to distance Vietnamese immigrants from criminality results in the re-criminalization of Blacks. The project that the authors in *Immigration and Crime* engage, which is to denaturalize immigrant criminality, ultimately results in reinforcing laddered boundaries between racial whiteness and racial Blackness, and an attempted negotiation, once again, to close the gap between the identities of "immigrant" and "American" becomes a violent act against Blacks.

Efforts to protect immigrants from violence such as deportation come from many venues, including the media. An analysis of some of the strategies employed by some *Los Angeles Times* reporters to defend immigrants' innocence reveals constructions between redeemable "good" immigrants—those that work hard and do not engage in crime—versus disposable "bad" immigrants—those that are lazy and engage in crime.[16]

---

16    Saito, 1998.

Ann M. Simmons, reporter for the *Los Angeles Times*, covered Jayantibhai and Indiraben Desai's story.[17] The couple, Jayantibhai, an Indian national, and Indiraben, a British national, overstayed their visas in the early 1980s and made their lives in the US, including raising their two children who attended college, a fact that was highlighted several times. Central to this discussion is Simmons's attempt to portray the Desais in a positive light by contrasting them with the hegemonic image of immigrants as public charges. In three different places within two articles Simmons makes the point that the Desais *pay taxes*, contrasting them with general notions that immigrants do not pay taxes and use resources. Simmons writes "For more than 20 years, the Norwalk couple worked hard. They bought a house, paid taxes and sent their two sons off to college. They were a success story in the making, but for one thing: Their status as illegal immigrants." She also includes these details more than once, attempting to further separate them from the image of public charge.

Implicit in Simmons's 2005 article is the attempt to distance the Desais from "criminals." The article is an attempt to answer questions of when and why immigrants are deported. She spends a significant amount of time discussing deportation based on issues of criminality and she argues that immigration policies are less forgiving now and she seems to imply that they are having negative effects on "deserving" families. Throughout her two articles she includes the fact that the Desais have two sons, both of whom are in college, which further constructs them as "deserving" immigrants. Simmons's discursive representation of the Desais reinforces contrasts between "good" and "bad" immigrants. The Desais are *different* from other immigrants. They are not "criminals" nor public charges, which Simmons seems to imply should give the Desais the ability to remain in the nation, in contrast to "criminals," who are implicitly undeserving and these *are* the people that should be targeted instead of these "good immigrants." Simmons writes that "The Desais' attorney, Carl Shusterman, said immigration judges used to be more forgiving of people who had put down roots in the United States, paid their taxes and proved themselves to be model members of society."[18] Through the analysis of Simmons's articles, a "good" immigrant is one who pays taxes, owns their own home, sends their children to college, and does not engage in "criminal" activity. These are the "deserving" immigrants who should be given special considerations, versus immi-

---

17 Ann M. Simmons, "Q&A/IMMIGRANTS AND DEPORTATION; Broad Range of Offenses Can Lead to Removal," *Los Angeles Times*, September 7, 2005: B.2; and "Deportation May Cut Short an Immigrant Success Story," *Los Angeles Times*, September 7, 29, 2004: B.4.

18 September 7, 2005.

grants who become public charges and engage in "criminal" activities.

Exemplary of this is another *Los Angeles Times* article by Patrick J. McDonnell.[19] McDonnell covers the story of Refugio Rubio who was arrested in 1972 for drug possession and served his sentence. Rubio attempted to obtain citizenship in large part because of the anti-immigrant backlash. Through his fingerprints, his 1972 conviction came up and set the stage for deportation. McDonnell describes Rubio as "A longtime field hand and laborer who has lived legally in the United States for almost 34 years, Rubio built his own home in the Bay Area community of Vallejo, and is the patriarch of a family that includes seven sons, all US citizens, and seven citizen grandchildren." In this example we see again the implicit contrast between "good" and "bad" immigrants. Rubio is described as hard working, self-sufficient, and having social ties to citizens. These two stories illustrate the impact that the language of welfare and public charge has on the immigration debate. In these cases the reporters attempt to portray the Desais and Rubio in a positive light by focusing on their family values, and the fact that they are not criminals.[20] McDonnell cites Rubio, "If I was a person who continued doing bad things, I could understand this ... But I never had trouble with the law again. I've always worked hard and paid my taxes, and my family has never depended on the government."

In these stories there is an explicit attempt to represent immigrants as "deserving," evidenced by the mentions of their status as home-owners, never being dependent on the state, working hard, and having children in college or who are "academically gifted." The debate attempting to defend immigrant rights is limited by the discussion of criminality and dependency. The articles suggest that those targeted are *upstanding* members of society, again rationalizing the violence that occurs to those that do not fit this category. However, there is a shift in the rhetoric of public charge. Critics have turned the rhetoric of public charge on its head by arguing that the process of detention is what becomes a public charge. However, this is limited to the "deserving" immigrants that advocates are willing to defend while either not engaging in the discussion of the deportation of people considered "criminal," rationalizing that the deportation of people considered "criminal" is justified, or in other occasions critiquing policies that have expanded what is considered "criminal" in order to expand the identity of "deserving" to a larger number of immigrants. One of the problems with engaging debates of immigration within

---

19    Patrick J. McDonnell, "Criminal Past Comes Back to Haunt Some Immigrants; Law: Legal residents now face deportation for crimes in US, no matter how old. Many insist they've reformed," *Los Angeles Times*, January 20, 1997: 1.

20    In Refugio Rubio's case, that he is rehabilitated.

this framework is that the binary opposition between "good" and "bad" immigrants necessarily naturalizes the exclusion of some, mostly immigrants labeled as "criminal" in order to defend the belonging of others. This naturalizes any negative effects on those that are deemed "criminal."

Furthermore, since "illegal immigrant" is fused with the identity of public charge, not only does the language of immigration conjure ideas of "illegality," but in addition it immediately evokes ideas of welfare and public charge, gendering the debate as female. For example, H.G. Reza's *Los Angeles Times* article, "Minor Offenders in Orange County Taken to Border Patrol," shows how the language of "illegality" is attached to the language of welfare. Reza discusses the practices of Orange County police officers profiling and stopping people that "look illegal," asking them for their papers and taking them to the San Clemente immigration checkpoint for deportation. Police argue that they are stopped for infractions such as "soliciting work or selling flowers on medians." In response to the critique that this is racial profiling and that this process is unconstitutional, the Orange County police denied these charges contending that "problems with people who are undocumented often warrant swift action, such as taking them directly to the checkpoint." They cited that they prefer to take them directly to the immigration checkpoint instead of booking them because "prosecuting a minor offense only to turn the convicted person over for deportation is costly." In other words, the costs of giving immigrants due process is viewed as too costly, and handing them over to the INS is understood as saving taxpayers' money. Again, the language of public charge is combined with "illegality" in order to rationalize anti-immigrant practices.

What the analysis of these news articles reveals is that discourse designed to discipline and contain Black bodies—criminality and state dependency—gets remapped onto migrant women, particularly of Mexican origin, and proves useful not only to discipline this group, but migrants in general. Fusing "criminality" and state dependency that occurred with the production of the welfare queen is proven productive to discipline immigrants into "good Americans." To claim innocence and belonging, immigrants have to renounce criminality and state dependency, ultimately renouncing Blackness.

Throughout this essay I examine criminality as a production that occurs around Black bodies, which results in the targeting of Black women's reproduction, and show how this patriarchal white supremacist discourse is re-mapped onto migrant women's bodies. As in the case of Black women, migrant women's reproduction is targeted to contain their "criminal" reproduction, exemplified through the passing of California's Proposition 187, the Welfare Reform Act, and IIRIRA. The immigrant rights discourse that attaches the identity of "migrant" to "hard worker" ultimately re-masculinizes migration and reinforces the exploitability of migrant bodies, enabling the regulation of both Black and brown women's productive and reproductive labor. The assumed criminality of these women's reproduction goes unchallenged. The discourse of criminality further serves to naturalize violence against both Black and brown bodies through the rhetoric of personal responsibility. On the one hand, migrants are assumed to "choose" to cross the border "illegally," and thus, whatever happens after this "criminal" act is self-made. On the other hand, Blacks are differentiated from migrants in part through US citizenship, and thus, impoverished Blacks who allegedly have more resources than migrants are also made personally responsible for their situation. In essence, their criminalization naturalizes violence, including state-inflicted violence as in the case of the ICE raids. The efforts of migrant rights advocates to claim migrant innocence is ultimately a negotiation between racial Blackness, perpetually detached from "American"-ness, and racial whiteness, a prerequisite for "American"-ness. By reinforcing "American"-ness, as is done when we claim "immigrants are not criminals, immigrants are hard workers," we essentially allow for patriarchal white supremacy to remain unchallenged and perpetuate the expendability of Black and brown. We need to move away from the idea "No One is Illegal," which conjures only migrant identities, to "No One is Criminal," which challenges patriarchal white supremacy.

MARTHA ESCOBAR *is a Ph.D. Candidate in Ethnic Studies at University of California, San Diego. She has accepted a dissertation fellowship with the US-Mexico Studies Center. She is a former chair of MECHA and has worked with Critical Resistance for the last seven years.*

# SAFER CITIES UNPLUGGED

*Pete White of the Los Angeles Community Action Network*

The Skid Row Safer City Initiative [SCI] is but a manifestation of an old, ingrained anti-poor and anti-minority sentiment that has permeated the fabric of life in the United States. Removing the veneer and holding accountable those who support the erosion of civil and human rights must be the first order of the day. Sadly enough, the most vocal supporters of this policing method look exactly like most of us who have been targeted by it. Mayor Villaraigosa, Councilmember Parks, Councilmember Perry and City Attorney Delgadillo must understand the price that we all pay when they grace the podium with words of support for the SCI. They must understand that in their moment of support they have ultimately supported the sentiment that led to lynching, castration, separation of family and community, degradation of women ... and the list goes on.

"We remain imprisoned by the past as long as we deny its influence in the present."

*Justice William Brennan*

Justice Brennan's quote is very timely when it comes to "unpacking" the real impetus driving the Skid Row Safer City Initiative [SCI]. This article attempts to connect the post-bellum journey of African-Americans leaving the manacles of slavery to their very similar experiences today. It attempts to shed light on the fact that the preservation of a certain pecking order is still the order of the day. It is a statement to the masses to organize or be organized. We have all heard the adage, "If we don't understand our history we will certainly repeat it" and it is our hope not to repeat it with SCI. While this maxim is most certainly true for the sum of us, the impact of not knowing our collective history is very different for those who currently find themselves at the bottom of the social pecking order.

Vagrancy laws—which happen to be the original name for today's quality-of-life policing strategy—have roots that extend as far back as 14th-century England. The original purpose was to create a substitute form of serfdom [slavery] by legislatively tying workers to the master's land. But by the middle of the 17th century, and up until the 19th century, the number of "masterless" men and families that crowded the streets led to a change of emphasis in vagrancy laws. The new thrust was to create methods of control and ways to banish those that were undesirable, financial burdens, nuisances, and potential criminals. Sound familiar?

Leaving England and making our way to the post-Civil War United States, we find other shining examples of vagrancy ordinances directed at the United States's favorite target, Black people. The utilization of Black Codes—vagrancy ordinances that were created by Southern legislators to retain control of their recently freed property—were used to discourage former slaves from leaving the "master's" plantation. It created a system where the likelihood of being arrested, charged, and punished far outweighed the risks of continued servitude.

While economic concerns were high on the white supremacy checklist, they were not the only concern. Next up on the list were the implications associated with scores of free, poor Black people roaming through White Communities, and what that would do to White people's "quality of life." To help us put into context the sentiment of the day, the following is an example of how Black vagrants were defined. This definition comes from Mississippi's Black Code, which reads:

> Runaways, drunkards, pilferers; lewd wanton, or lascivious [exciting lust] persons, in speech or behavior; those who neglect their employment, misspend their earnings, and fail to support their families; and all idle and disorderly persons.

The definition was also applied to white people who threatened the "white way of life." Association with Black people in any way that suggested equality, or being found guilty of having sexual relations with them, was a quick way to get caught up in the vagrancy dragnet. From the late 1860s through the 1960s, states created harsher and stiffer vagrancy laws which were written in a very detailed manner. However, they allowed for broad and ambiguous interpretation. These laws served as the essential tool of defining and policing the racial landscape.

## REVERSING THE VAGRANCY MOVEMENT

The first landmark decision falling on the side of the oppressed was *Shuttlesworth v. City of Birmingham*. In this case the Birmingham Police Department charged a Black civil rights advocate [Shuttlesworth] with vagrancy simply because he was picketing in front of a department store that was discriminating against Black employees. Shuttlesworth was subsequently sentenced to 241 days of hard labor. The Supreme Court eventually dismissed the charges against Shuttlesworth stating:

> Literally read, ... [speaking of the vagrancy ordinance] says that a person may stand on a public sidewalk in Birmingham only at the whim of any police officer of that city ... Instinct with its ever-present potential for arbitrarily suppressing First Amendment liberties, that kind of law bears the hallmark of a police state.

Utilizing the momentum built in *Shuttlesworth v. City of Birmingham* the Supreme Court dealt another temporary death-blow to quality-of-life advocates when it rendered its opinion in *Papachristou v. City of Jacksonville*. This case was brought as a result of Florida police officers pulling over four motorists—two white women and two Black men—and charging them with vagrancy. Florida argued that vagrancy statutes should be allowed because they have the chilling effect of stopping crime before it starts (broken windows language used today), suggesting that crime was imminent between this colorful cast of daters. However, the Supreme Court worried that broadly-worded statutes possessed the real danger of potentially harassing and controlling minority groups.

The Court opinioned:

> Those generally implicated by the imprecise terms of the ordinance—poor people, non-conformists, dissenters, idlers—may be required to comport themselves according to the lifestyle deemed appropriate by the Jacksonville police and the courts. Where, as here, there are no standards governing the exercise of the discretion granted by the ordinance, the scheme ... furnishes a convenient tool for "harsh and discriminatory enforcement by local prosecuting officials, against particular groups deemed to merit their displeasure." It results in a regime in which the poor and the unpopular are permitted to "stand on a public sidewalk ... only at the whim of any police officer.

While these occurrences happened in the 1960s, they could have just as easily happened yesterday or the day before. In many respects the same occurrences are happening on a daily basis in downtown's Skid Row, where everyone who is a darker shade of Brown is being profiled for the crimes they could potentially commit. In a recent public meeting, an officer said that they sometimes arrest people for their own safety. I can only wonder what the Supreme Court would have to say about that one.

## BROKEN WINDOWS [SAFER CITY INITIATIVE] OR THE RETURN OF STATE-SANCTIONED REPRESSION?

James Q. Wilson and Dr. George Kelling signaled the return of post-bellum policing of America's ghettos, plus, a new way to get around the *Papachristou v. City of Jacksonville* opinion. In their March 1982 *Atlantic Monthly* article entitled "Broken Windows: The Police and Neighborhood Safety," Wilson and Kelling singlehandedly created the movement to employ a community policing model based in the old vagrancy framework. They explicitly argued that broad police discretion is necessary for effective enforcement even if that discretion leads to some infringement of civil rights. The authors note, "Arresting a single drunk or a single vagrant who has harmed no identifiable person seems unjust, and in a sense it is. But failing to do anything about a score of drunks or a hundred vagrants may destroy an entire community."

One can further ascertain the focus and spirit of the broken windows duo by reading Wilson's quote from his book *Varieties of Police Behavior* (1968). Wilson states:

> A noisy drunk, a rowdy teenager shouting or racing his car in the middle of the night, a loud radio in the apartment next door, a panhandler soliciting money from passersby, persons wearing eccentric clothes and unusual hair styles loitering in public places—all these are examples of behavior which the "public" (an onlooker, a neighbor, the community at large) may disapprove of (1968: 16).

He goes on to say:

> A teenager hanging out on a street corner late at night, especially one dressed in eccentric manner, a Negro wearing a "conk rag" (a piece of cloth tied around the head to hold flat hair being "processed"—that is straightened), girls in shorts and boys in long hair parked in a flashy car talking loudly to friends on the curb, or interracial couples—all of these are seen by many police officers as persons displaying unconventional and improper behavior (1968:39-40).

Bernard Harcourt—one of the broken window theory's most vocal critics—has written extensively on the "cracks" that exist in the theory. In addition to writing, he has spoken at great length on the subject matter, calling on Kelling, Bratton, and other broken windows proponents to debate their success. For example, on March 15, 2006, Kelling was asked by "Good Day Colorado" (KDVR-TV) to discuss the policing strategy (Denver, Colorado is another city that is implementing broken windows policing). What Kelling did not know was that "Good Day Colorado" had also asked Bernard Harcourt to provide the opposing viewpoint. After the anchor introduced Kelling—who was more than willing to be the expert—he was abruptly interrupted by Kelling who insisted he was not willing to debate the matter with Harcourt. The reporter wanted to know why, if this was such a sound theory, he would not debate it publicly and to that Kelling hung up. This was all done during a live news broadcast. I will let you figure out what that really means.

The bottom line is that broken windows policing is in itself broken. It is blatantly based in racist policies used from the 1860s to the 1960s, many of which were overturned by the Courts. The authors themselves won't publicly defend their own theory. Yet, the City of Los Angeles has paid one of the authors, George Kelling, over $450,000 to craft and implement broken windows policing focused right now on the Skid Row community. Angelenos who believe in racial justice and the protection of civil and human rights must act. Join LA CAN in holding the Mayor and City Council accountable and ending broken windows policing downtown and throughout L.A. We can and will defend ourselves.

*The mission of the LOS ANGELES COMMUNITY ACTION NETWORK (LA CAN) is to help people dealing with poverty create and discover opportunities, while serving as a vehicle to ensure they have voice, power, and opinion in the decisions that are directly affecting them. We were founded in response to the mass criminalization of addiction, mental illness, and poverty so prevalent in our community and the devastating impacts of these policies. While our focus remains on civil/human rights and preventing criminalization, we have added projects over the years addressing housing policy, economic development, health and nutrition, violence prevention, and gender equity.*

## REFERENCES

Wilson, James Q. 1991. "Character and Community: The Problem with Broken Windows." *On Character*. Washington, D.C.: AEI Press.

Wilson, James Q. 1968. *Varieties of Police Behavior*. Cambridge: Harvard University Press.

# A CANADIAN JOURNEY INTO ABOLITION

*Kim Pate*

Penal reform is tantamount to rearranging the deck chairs on the Titanic. When we talk about law reform, in terms of where we are now, we must work very hard to stem the tsunami-like tide of women, particularly poor, racialized, victimized women, into our prisons.

Women are the fastest growing prison population worldwide. This is not accidental. In Canada, and many other western countries, we are seeing the increased criminalization and institutionalization of women, as well as their advocates and allies. Our link to the United States has meant that we are impacted by the globalized capitalist lunges for cash and products, which are occasioning the destruction of social safety nets—from social and health services to economic and education standards and availability. The result is the virtual inevitability of criminalization, as laws and policies are increasingly coming into conflict with peoples' lives.

For example, by creating extremely low welfare rates and bans on receipt of state resources, many poor people are relegated to a criminalized underclass. In 1996, the Canadian government eliminated the Canada Assistance Plan and therefore the essential nature of Canadian standards of social, medical, and educational resourcing. Canadians have now experienced all sorts of cuts and knee-jerk, band aid responses—all of which presume criminality and perpetuate the feminization and criminalization of poverty.

Perhaps the most graphic and tragic example of the intersection of federal and regional economic, social, financial, health, and education issues, is the death of

Kim Rogers, a forty-year-old woman we (the Canadian Association of Elizabeth Fry Societies) knew well, a woman who was set up to fail.

Ontario, the same province that created violently irresponsible welfare rates, chose to prosecute Kim for receiving welfare payments while she attempted to get an education. Kim was unable to work at her usual job because of a disabling knee injury. During the inquest following her death, we discovered that she would likely have been eligible to attend school while on "disability welfare," but neither she nor her worker were aware of this option. As such, when she chose to attend school because she could do her usual bartending and waitressing work, she was deemed to be violating her responsibility to be looking for work. In addition, Kim was further vilified because she received student loans to help pay for her education.

Although it is impossible to live on welfare anywhere in Canada without supplemental income/support, to be caught attempting to patch together a sustainable income means almost certain criminal prosecution. Kim entered a guilty plea and was consequently convicted of "welfare fraud." She was sentenced to pay back money she had received from the state as social assistance, student loans, and even monies that were originally characterized as "grants." She was also sentenced to serve six months of house arrest, jailed in her own home. Not only should she never have been criminalized in the first place, why should a jail sentence be attached to this "offense" at all?

We must interfere with these draconian, destructive, and illegal practices. How can someone sentenced to jail in her home support herself and her children? Too many of those labeled as "offenders" in these contexts are single and sole support Moms, yet the State gets away with permanently barring them from obtaining social assistance. These policies constitute a complete and utter set-up —a set-up to which the judge, prosecutor, and defense counsel were all privy when it happened to Kim. Kim died, eight months pregnant, during a heat wave in August 2001. The police registered a temperature of 35–39 degrees Celsius when they entered her apartment at 8pm the day they believe she died. Moreover, even after Kim's death, and although a legal challenge resulted in the reinstatement of her "benefits," the Ontario government continued to enforce its policy to terminate benefits and permanently disentitle anyone convicted of "welfare fraud" from receiving welfare.

Who says there is no war against the most dispossessed, especially the poor?

We must stop criminalizing poor women for welfare fraud, prostitution, drug trafficking, and other things that they choose or may be forced to do in order to survive in increasingly inhospitable surroundings. Criminalizing poor women stamps them as somehow dangerous to the general public, but the fact is, if we are truly interested in addressing actions that harm others, then politicians and policymakers who mandate unsustainable welfare rates should be our targets. Those responsible for and/or complicit in the destruction of our social safety net are in the greatest need of "correction."

We should challenge the creation of laws and policies that effectively criminalize poverty, disabilities, and the resisters of colonization. We must challenge classifications, assessments, and "correction" tools that train ordinary people to believe that the individuals sucked or thrown into the prison industrial complex are there because of planned, voluntary, and criminally intended actions.

In addition, the so called "war on drugs" has become a war on the dispossessed, especially women who use, sell, or otherwise deal in legal or illegal drugs in order to cope with everyday life and/or to gain the financial resources they need for survival. Our public policies demand that women and girls avoid one of the few behaviours that allow them to diminish the pain of poverty, abuse, and disabilities, in the face of profoundly inadequate income, housing, medical, educational resources, and other supports.

After being imprisoned, women and girls are released, having been dosed with psycho-social, cognitive skills, or drug abstinence programming and sent forth with the official judgment that they are in control of and therefore responsible for their own lives, including their own criminalization. We absolutely reject and resist such notions.

It is difficult to talk or write about our work without feeling both extreme despair and outrage. Indeed, I find that much of my work and actions is driven by emotions that vacillate between the two. Part of the difficulty in addressing the issues that are increasingly arising for women prisoners in Canada and internationally, is the reality that things are supposed to have improved significantly since the bleak days when Canada had only one federal prison for women.

It is now almost twenty years since *Creating Choices* (Report of the Task Force on Federally Sentenced Women) was accepted by the Correctional Service of Canada (CSC), just over twelve years since the first of the new women's prisons opened and Madam Justice Arbour issued her scathing indictment of the manner in which the CSC manages corrections, the imprisonment of women in particular. On July 6th, 2000, we finally celebrated the closure of the Prison for Women, ending its sixty-six-year history of confining women and girls.

For federally sentenced women, CAEFS, and many others, it was a muted celebration. The Prison for Women was replaced by ten other federal prison units for women; eleven, counting the now replaced provincial prison for women in British Columbia, the Burnaby Correctional Centre for Women. Four of these were segregated maximum security units in men's prisons. One remains open. Three have been closed, but replaced by five new segregated super-max prisons for women within the walls of the regional prisons. The number of women serving federal prison terms has almost tripled since the tabling of *Creating Choices*. It is no wonder that women prisoners frequently ask: "Whatever happened to Creating Choices?"

It is vital to know that although *Creating Choices* was heralded as the pinnacle of penal reform, the report represented a compromise position for our organization, other community groups, and especially the women in and from prison.

So, twenty years after what many have described as the most progressive penal reform initiative internationally, how far have we come? Within one year of the tabling of the *Creating Choices*, the community and prisoner members of the Task Force were mostly eliminated from the implementation process, as one by one they were cut out of the process. No doubt only because of the suicides of six Aboriginal women in Prisons for Women, the last group to be extinguished was the Aboriginal women who formed the Vision Circle for the Okimaw Ohci Healing Lodge, the national prison for First Nations, Métis, and Inuit women.

When Madam Justice Louise Arbour issued her report, the Commission of Inquiry into Certain Events at the Prison for Women in Kingston, on April 1, 1996, she indicted the prison industrial complex:

> In terms of general correctional issues, the facts of this inquiry have revealed a disturbing lack of commitment to the ideals of justice on the part of the Correctional Service. I firmly believe that increased judicial supervision is required. The two areas in which the Service has been the most delinquent are the management of segregation and administration of the grievance process. In both areas, the deficiencies that the facts have revealed were serious and detrimental to prisoners in every respect, including in undermining their rehabilitative prospects. There is nothing to suggest that the Service is either willing or able to reform without judicial guidance and control. (Commission of Inquiry into Certain Events at the Prison for Women in Kingston, *The Arbour Commission Report, 1996: 198*).

According to CSC statistics, 82% of the women in federal prisons are serving their first federal sentence, and only 1.6% of the women have experienced three or more terms of imprisonment. Lifers comprise 22% of the federal women's population. 4% of the women serving federal sentences were convicted of first degree murder, and 14% for second degree murder. Approximately 44% of the women serving federal sentences are racialized women, about 30% are Aboriginal, 6% are African Canadian, 1% identify as South Asian, and the rest are described as "uncategorized." Fifty-two percent of all federally sentenced women and 83% of federally sentenced women labeled as "maximum security" are under the age of thirty-five; and, depending upon the day, 40-60% will be Aboriginal women in the segregated maximum security setting. All of the women designated as super-maximum security pursuant to the CSC's "management protocol" are Aboriginal women.

Prison authorities are labeling ever-higher numbers of young women as pathologically ill, and as suffering from mental illness. If a woman is poor, racialized and officially diagnosed as "mentally ill," she is more likely to be sent to prison today than to a psychiatric or mental health facility. Older, progressive ideas about de-institutionalization have died away; now people are being dumped into the streets.

Women are labeled as bearers of Fetal Alcohol Spectrum Disorder (FASD), "borderline personality," and other catch-all diagnoses. Once in prison, these women tend to be characterized by the Correctional Service of Canada as among the most difficult prisoners to manage, so authorities classify them, disproportionately, as maximum security prisoners, housing them during the majority of their sentences in segregated maximum security units in men's prisons. Such conditions of confinement only exacerbate pre-existing mental health issues. Moreover, the levels of isolation and consequent sensory deprivation tend to create additional mental health issues.

Ironically, the odious reflex of CSC to develop mental health services in prisons only worsens the trend to criminalize women with mental and cognitive disabilities. Developing such services in prisons, at a time when they are increasingly non-existent in the community, justifies federal sentences for more women with the argument that they can access services in prison that are not available in community settings. The result is that women are entering prisons with significant needs, but prisons are not and cannot be treatment centers.

We are seeing a direct relationship between such policies and the increased criminalization of the most marginalized, especially young, racialized, and poor women. This is a significant part of the reason that we co-hosted *Women's Resistance: From Victimization to Criminalization* with the Canadian Association of Sexual Assault Centres in October, 2001. The conference created an unprecedented opportunity for women in and from prisons, rape crisis centers, and women's shelters, front-line anti-prison and anti-violence workers, lawyers, academics, politicians, bureaucrats, and other professionals to come together to work on strategies to further women's equality. The conference focused on these issues, welfare policies, and the ongoing struggle against attacks on the poor and criminalization of the most dispossessed.

Contemporary anti-violence policies and practices are also harming women. Fewer women are willing today to try to seek protection from misogynist violence by invoking the power of the state, in part because so-called gender neutral, zero tolerance policies, are being used to counter-charge women. We are also seeing counsel advising women who've felt they have no choice but to use lethal force to defend themselves and/or their children, to plead guilty to either second degree murder or manslaughter. In fact, when Judge Ratushny conducted the Self Defence Review, she found that approximately twenty to thirty of the women serving federal sentences in relation to the deaths of abusive partners had entered guilty pleas and therefore precluded their cases from review.

Despite these grim realities, those of us who work with and are allied with women prisoners know very well that those women continue to call upon all of us to do our utmost to ensure that their voices are brought out from behind the walls. It is as a result of their continued perseverance that the rest of us are afforded the privilege of being able to continue to walk with them as they challenge the manner in which they are held captive and imprisoned in Canada.

On International Women's Day, March 8, 2001, after years of attempting to negotiate with CSC to implement the recommendations of the Arbour report and the provisions of the *Corrections and Conditional Release Act* (CCRA), the Canadian Association of Elizabeth Fry Societies (CAEFS) and the Native Women's Association of Canada filed a complaint with the Canadian Human Rights Commission. As a result, the Commission decided to conduct a broad-based systemic review of the situation experienced by federally sentenced women, utilizing its authority pursuant to s.61(2) of the *Canadian Human Rights Act* to report on the manner in which the Government of Canada is discriminating against women serving prison sentences of two years or more.

The CAEFS's complaint articulated, among other issues, that unlike their male counterparts, with the exception of ten beds that have been slated for closure, women who are classified as minimum security prisoners do not have access to minimum security prisons. Furthermore, despite the promises of *Creating Choices* and the CCRA, there are insufficient community-based releasing options for women, especially Aboriginal women. Similarly, in addition to being subjected to a discriminatory classification scheme, women classified as maximum security prisoners and those identified as having cognitive and mental disabilities are not provided with adequate or appropriate carceral placement options. The Commission confirmed that the Canadian government is breaching the human rights of women prisoners by discrimination on the basis of sex, race, and disability.

Canada prides itself on its international human rights reputation. When it comes to the manner in which we treat our most marginalized, that reputation is too often unwarranted. Consequently, we have also taken these issues to the United

Nations. The UN Human Rights Committee, as well as a number of Special Rapporteurs and other international bodies, have critiqued the Canadian government's refusal to implement the recommendations of the Arbour Commission or even the repeated recommendations of their own Correctional Service of Canada. The CSC's task forces on federally sentenced women and segregation called for external oversight, as well as its own commission's recommendations for judicial oversight. The CSC has even rejected the recommendations of the Parliamentary Standing Committee on Justice and Human Rights on this point.

Imagine the results if Canadians decided to ensure that every prisoner learned about the history of the use of criminal law to colonize Aboriginal peoples in order to separate them from their land and culture. What if the government endorsed education for all prisoners about the criminalization of the indigent and homeless through laws prohibiting vagrancy and night walking, while simultaneously failing to condemn the abuse of power and force by police and prison personnel, and the neglect of institutionalized persons?

Imagine if we chose to reject current theories of crime and criminality and instead chose to focus on trying to prevent—and, when unsuccessful punish—those who perpetrate the most harmful behaviors: those who wage war. Why hasn't Bush been indicted for war crimes or crimes against humanity? What about those who hoard essential goods, make excess profits, irresponsibly and negligently handle toxic cargo, crimes against social harmony, economic and/or even governmental order? What would the system look like if we prosecuted and sentenced people for lying while running for office, wrongful use or access to government power and public resources?

Too many of us spend our time vibrating between rage and despair as we strive to act in ways that will directly benefit and change the status quo for those most oppressed. Let's use that anger to fuel our action, but let's not stop there. Let's also remember to celebrate our resisters and revolutionary thinkers and doers.

Depending on where we stand, our projects may differ somewhat. In Canada, we urge focus on the Aboriginal women who, by forcing international focus on inadequate housing and other basic human rights on Reserves, and on poisoned land and water, have taken our federal government to the United Nations, causing Canada to lose its #1 world rating regarding the standard of living of citizens.

We urge focus on the workers who led the Winnipeg general strike and other labor leaders who helped define a humane work week—and, equally importantly, helped secure our weekends. We would toast the working class feminist organizers who insisted that women and children no longer be considered the property of the men who sired or married them, who insisted that violence against women and children must no longer be tolerated, while hiding those same women from the men who tried to kill them and their kids.

We would follow the young people who demand that we fight globalization and capitalism, the students in Quebec who went on strike a few years ago to fight the increased privatization of prisons, healthcare and education and corresponding cuts to public funding of education and other essential services, the First Nations who blockade highways and logging roads to draw attention to the rape of the land, Canada's pledge to Aboriginal women and women's groups who for 20 years refused to accept "never" as an answer as they demanded and ensured that 500 missing and murdered Aboriginal women in Canada did not continue to be abandoned by the criminal injustice system and the penal industrial machine.

We should also honour the lawyers, who were sued, in addition to being censured by their so-called professional colleagues, and nearly lost their livelihood when they labeled the racism of the police after they strip-searched three 12 year old girls in a school. (The bully-boy tactics were also employed against Corinne Sparks, the African Nova Scotian judge who took judicial notice of the racism of police). And, the many youth, men, and especially the women prisoners who refuse to succumb, who will not stand-down or over, but instead walk with their sisters inside … like the ones who courageously authorized the release of information to the media about what has now come to be known as "the April 1994 incident," when eight women, five of whom are Aboriginal, were illegally stripped, shackled, transferred to a men's prison, then were held for 9 months in isolation until the videotape of the degrading, humiliating, and illegal treatment they suffered was broadcast around the world!

By focusing on initiatives to keep women in the community and facilitate their integration after prison, our member societies work to encourage the Canadian public to embrace abolition and decarceration. Particularly in this time of fiscal restraint, our aim is to retain a proactive focus in order to encourage the development of, and support for, community-based options, rather than pay the human and fiscal costs of our increasing reliance on incarceration. We focus on increasing public awareness of the myriad issues facing women in prison and gradually break down the stereotypes of criminalized women.

The CAEFS continues to challenge Canadians to reach behind the walls and welcome women into the communities, so that they may take responsibility and account for their actions in ways that enhance our national, provincial, and local commitment and adherence to fundamental principles of equality and justice. We think that current international realities demand that we expand our coalition to end imprisonment, making common cause with activists around the world. We could easily start with women and girls. Just think about what we might achieve if our individual countries alone, let alone collectively and globally, manage to de-carcerate women. We could see reinvestment in community development, women's services and women's equality of resources freed up as a result of prison closures. In turn, this could lead to the decarceration of men.

We look forward to working on this international agenda with you. Indeed, as our allies in and from prison often remind us, the words of an Australian Ab-original woman named Lilla Watson best encapsulate and convey the message of our work:

> If you have come here to help me,
> you are wasting our time.
> If you have come here because
> your liberation is bound up with mine,
> then let us work together.

For copies of CAEFS's position papers or additional information, please contact Kim Pate directly at kpate@web.ca, visit the CAEFS's home page at http://www.elizabethfry.ca, telephone us at (613) 238-2422, or fax us at (613) 232-7130.

KIM PATE, *mother to Michael and Madison, has had the privilege and respon-sibility of working in alliance with marginalized, victimized, criminalized, and institutionalized youth, men, and women for the past twenty-five years. Her current waged work is with the Canadian Association of Elizabeth Fry Societies (CAEFS). CAEFS is an abolitionist group focused on fighting all forms of oppres-sion with a view to achieving substantive equality for women and girls in Canada and internationally.*

# SURVIVING WARFARE, PRACTICING RESISTANCE

*Pilar Maschi, interviewed by David Stein*

The "war on drugs" is a feature of the prison industrial complex (PIC) that continues to have a remarkable impact on who gets surveilled, arrested, tried, convicted, and imprisoned, and how those processes unfold. In what follows, Pilar Maschi, long-time organizer with Critical Resistance reflects on her personal experiences with substance use and the abolitionist potentials for engaging drug users compassionately. Pilar spoke with David Stein of The CR10 Publications Collective about the practice of resistance within the warfare of the PIC.

DAVID: How do you see the drug war as an integral piece to the PIC?

PILAR: The drug war. [That] title has always kind of thrown me off a little bit just because I think it's hard to think about ... We could use a different word or term. The drug war ... what does that mean?

DAVID: I would say what gets called "the drug war" is more accurately the way in which a scare around certain people using narcotics has been used to police mainly Black and brown communities and to lock Black and brown communities in cages over the past thirty years, and then for the government to then like spray coca crops throughout the Global South, you know, so I don't have a term to identify that other than you know fascism ...

But it [is] also this important piece to the story of the last twenty-five to thirty years of imprisonment in the US.

PILAR: Definitely. A lot longer, too.

DAVID: How do you see, what gets called the "drug war" or the "war on drugs" being deployed as part of the PIC?

PILAR: It is really clever. Obviously, it's used to lock our people up. When I started using and people found out about it, people looked at me in a very, very different way, you know what I mean? People would not leave their wallet around. These are my best friends. I wouldn't be invited to their houses, like all of the sudden I was stealing shit. I had diseases, I was dying, I was a prostitute—I was all these things. It's really degrading.

[The PIC] makes like all these things, the way that we survive, like we're just really bad people. We're like at the low totem pole, we're like the lowest. If you're an addict, you're abandoned by your community. You're just looked at like garbage. You're not trusted. I was also supported by some of those people in my community too, but the majority—they say you're looking a little different, walking a little fast, looking a little dirty, you know? And then there's the obvious, also. People see you around; you're on the street a lot, homeless. The cops see you—they're going to target you. That's pretty much where I got my rap sheet, how I got my record. My criminal record is from drugs. I've been in jail, in a women's facility, the majority of us [were] addicts.

And how it impacts us: locking us up, putting us in cages directly is one. Two, the way that we're seen in the street, and in the mainstream and the media, even by our own people, is really messed up and demoralizing and it hurts us and puts us into isolation even more as addicts. And three, our family members. Everybody in our community is hurt and traumatized by all this.

And the state violence that happens to us as addicts. Our kids are affected by it, you know what I mean? There [are] so many women and men, also fathers, that are locked up right now that have lost total custody of their children. Some will not see their children again because of getting locked up for addiction. If you have children and you're locked up, where's that kid going to go? A lot of kids go into foster care. Kids are not going to see their parents. It's just not something I feel like people should be criminalized for at all.

I like harm reduction. I think we need to be really honest; we're not necessarily going to get rid of drugs. At this point in time pharmaceutical companies are the biggest drug dealers of them all. They're actually wiping out the street drug dealers. As long as we have despair and all these feelings, and people get high for those reasons, it's a real thing. So how do we take care of our people who are using to an extreme, where they're hurting themselves and they're hurting the ones that they love? When that happens, how do we really deal with that and really heal and stop it? [How do we] stop hurting each other in a way that is loving, community-led, and community-driven, not state-driven?

DAVID: How does recovery and survival relate to an abolitionist practice?

PILAR: Recovery and survival. Recovery and survival. As an abolitionist, recovery is not only about healing from the symptoms of being drugged. To me, one of the things that saved my life is resistance and being able to have a voice as an individual that has managed to survive until this day. That is something that has kept me in a place where I'm taking care of my child, I'm somewhat healthy, I'm able to give back or even just help build our community to a point where we're not relying on police or prisons. And that's giving space; making our organizing accessible to everybody, meaning addicts as well, and that's a tough one for some people.

I felt like I didn't have a voice; I gave up. A lot of that was the reason why I was an addict in the first place and started using hard-core drugs. And seeing that then there's a community, and back then it wasn't really a movement to me, it was a community of folks, when I heard about CR. [I was] like, "Oh shit, they don't like police, they don't like the state or the government." They don't think [the police are] doing a good thing. And. "Wow, they got my back." Recovery is really necessary, and I'm not talking about just addiction, I'm talking about recovery from the trauma that we have from state violence period, from the present that we have with cops beating down on people. We see this everyday. In my neighborhood, it's a very common thing. It's definitely not far off in another world. We have to recover everyday from this violence, and harassment and all this shit.

As an abolitionist, we organize and then that's one piece of doing the work. But I also feel like we need to provide some stuff. We need to really be intentional about sharing the skills that we have, the resources that we have as individuals and as our organization and our movement for people that might not have access to that stuff. We really need to learn to live beyond surviving. That's going to decrease us from doing harm to each other.

I guess the burning need that I have that I really want to share [as an] abolitionist, [is] it's okay to be really honest with each other and be really honest with yourself and not pretend or not hold yourself up to this expectation where you feel that you need to be 100% abolitionist like, "I have to do everything right." But [to] recognize that we're all human and that this is a life-long process. Everyday. Like allowing [ourselves] the freedom to be human and allowing us as individuals and abolitionists, to look at people [and go] beyond talking about it. I want to really to be able to build relationships with people and really understand where the hell they're coming from before I judge and assume that this person is a certain way because they look a certain way. I wish we could really be honest with each other and work through that. If folks are honest and real, [about having] judgments and assumptions, we'd be able to challenge ourselves [about] thinking in those boxes. I feel like we need to challenge that within our organizing as abolitionists, straight-up. Because how are we going to challenge the state if we can't even challenge each other?

*To read or hear more from* **PILAR MASCHI** *on the relationship between drug use, recovery, and abolition, please see Beyond Media's website: http://womenandprison. org/social-justice/pilar-maschi.html for additional remarks.*

# "WARFARE AND THE TERMS OF ENGAGEMENT"

*Dylan Rodríguez*

## INTRODUCTION: WARFARE AND THE TERMS OF ENGAGEMENT

As I've said before, we've taken down the surrender flag and run up the battle flag. And we're going to win the war on drugs.

*Pres. Ronald Reagan,*
*Radio Address to the Nation on Federal Drug Policy, October 2, 1982*

My generation will remember how America swung into action when we were attacked in World War II. The war was not just fought by the fellows flying the planes or driving the tanks. It was fought at home by a mobilized nation—men and women alike—building planes and ships, clothing sailors and soldiers, feeding marines and airmen; and it was fought by children planting victory gardens and collecting cans. Well, now we're in another war for our freedom, and it's time for all of us to pull together again.

In this crusade, let us not forget who we are. Drug abuse is a repudiation of everything America is. The destructiveness and human wreckage mock our heritage. Think for a moment how special it is to be an American. Can we doubt that only a divine providence placed this land, this island of freedom, here as a refuge for all those people on the world who yearn to breathe free?

*Pres. Ronald Reagan,*
*Address to the Nation on the Campaign Against Drug Abuse, September 14, 1986*

This war is not yet won, not by a long shot.

When we say zero tolerance, we mean, simply, that we've had it. We will no longer tolerate those who sell drugs and those who buy drugs. All Americans of good will are determined to stamp out those parasites who survive and even prosper by feeding off the energy and vitality and humanity of others. They must pay.

That's why the administration ... has advocated tougher measures than ever before to combat the drug runners and the drug dealers. We're doing this by seizing the ill-gotten possessions of drug dealers and their accomplices. Those fancy cars and fancy houses and bank accounts full of dirty money aren't really theirs. They were bought from the sale of illegal blood pollutants. We do not tolerate companies that poison our harbors and rivers, and we won't let people who are poisoning the blood of our children get away with it either.

Those who have the gall to use federally subsidized housing to peddle their toxins must get the message as well. We will not tolerate those who think they can do their dirty work in the same quarters where disadvantaged Americans struggle to build a better life. We want to kick the vermin out and keep them out.

*Pres. Ronald Reagan,*
*Radio Address to the Nation on Economic Growth and the War on Drugs,*
*October 8, 1988*

We give up freedom when we addict ourselves to drugs. This fact is not lost on the terrorists.

*Asa Hutchinson, Administrator, Drug Enforcement Administration,*
*"The Past, Present, & Future of the War on Drugs," November 15, 2001*

This introductory litany of dread reminds us that *domestic* warfare is both the common language and intensely materialized modality of the US state. While this form of legitimated state violence certainly predates Reagan's "war on drugs" and his/its inheritors, the scope and depth of domestic warmaking seems to be mounting with a peculiar urgency in our historical moment. To take former NYPD and current LAPD Chief William Bratton on the strength of his own words, the primary work of the police is to engage aggressively in "the internal war on terrorism," which in these times entails everything from record-breaking expansions of urban police forces, to cross-party consensus in legislating state offensives against criminalized populations of choice, and the reshuffling of administrative relationships between the militarized and juridical arms of local and federal government to facilitate the state's various localized "wars on gangs." It is in this context that we can urgently assume the political burden of critically assessing the work of progressive US based community and non-profit organizations, grassroots movements, and issue-based campaigns: that is, if we are to take the state's *own language* of domestic warfare seriously, what do we make of the political, ideological, institutional, and financial relationships that progressive movements, campaigns, and organizations are creating *in (uneasy) alliance with* the state's vast architectures of war? Under what conditions and sets of assumptions are progressive activists, organizers, and scholars able to so militantly oppose the proliferation of American state violence in other parts of the world, while tolerating the everyday state violence of US policing, criminal law, and low-intensity genocide?

We are collectively witnessing, surviving, and working in a time of unprecedented state-organized human capture and state-produced physical/social/psychic alienation, from the 2.5 million imprisoned by the domestic and global US prison industrial complex to the profound forms of informal apartheid and proto-apartheid that are being instantiated in cities, suburbs, and rural areas all over the country. This condition presents a profound crisis—and political possibility—for people struggling against the white supremacist state, which continues to institutionalize the social liquidation and physical evisceration of Black, brown, and aboriginal peoples nearby and far away. If we are to approach racism, neoliberalism, militarism/militarization, and US state hegemony and domination in a legitimately "global" way, it is nothing short of unconscionable to expend significant political energy protesting American wars elsewhere (e.g. Iraq, Afghanistan, etc.) when there are overlapping, and *no less profoundly oppressive*, declarations of and mobilizations for war in our very own, most intimate and nearby geographies of "home."

This time of crisis and emergency necessitates a critical examination of the political and institutional logics that structure so much of the US progressive left, and particularly the "establishment" left that is tethered (for better and worse) to the non-profit industrial complex (NPIC). I have defined the NPIC elsewhere as the set of symbiotic relationships that link political and financial technologies of state and owning class social control with surveillance over public political discourse, including and especially emergent progressive and leftist social movements. This definition is most focused on the industrialized incorporation, accelerated since the 1970s, of pro-state liberal and progressive campaigns and movements into a spectrum of government-proctored non-profit organizations.

It is in the context of the formation of the NPIC as a political power structure that I wish to address, with a less-than-subtle sense of alarm, a peculiar and disturbing *politics of assumption* that often structures, disciplines, and actively shapes the work of even the most progressive movements and organizations within the US establishment left (of which I too am a part, for better and worse): that is, the left's willingness to fundamentally tolerate—*and accompanying unwillingness to abolish*—the institutionalized dehumanization of the contemporary policing and imprisonment apparatus in its most localized, unremarkable, and hence "normal" manifestations within the domestic "homeland" of the Homeland Security state.

Behind the din of progressive and liberal reformist struggles over public policy, civil liberties, and law, and beneath the infrequent mobilizations of activity to defend against the next onslaught of racist, classist, ageist, and misogynist criminalization, there is an unspoken politics of assumption that *takes for granted* the mystified permanence of domestic warfare as a constant production of targeted and massive suffering, guided by the logic of Black, brown, and indigenous subjection to the expediencies and essential violence of the American (global) nation-building project. To put it differently: despite the unprecedented forms of imprisonment, social and political repression, and violent policing that compose the mosaic of our historical time, the establishment left (within and perhaps beyond the US) does not care to envision, much less politically prioritize, the *abolition of US domestic warfare* and its structuring white supremacist social logic as its most urgent task of the present and future. Our non-profit left, in particular, seems content to engage in desperate (and usually well-intentioned) attempts to *manage the casualties* of domestic warfare, foregoing the urgency of an abolitionist praxis that openly, critically, and radically addresses the moral, cultural, and political premises of these wars.

Not long from now, generations will emerge from the organic accumulation of rage, suffering, social alienation, and (we hope) politically principled rebellion against this living apocalypse and pose to us some rudimentary questions of radical accountability: How were we able to accommodate, and even culturally and politically *normalize* the strategic, explicit, and openly racist technologies of state violence that effectively socially neutralized and frequently liquidated entire *nearby* populations of our people, given that ours are the very same populations that have historically struggled to survive and overthrow such "classical" structures of dominance as colonialism, frontier conquest, racial slavery, and other genocides? In a somewhat more intimate sense, *how could we live with ourselves* in this domestic state of emergency, and why did we seem to generally forfeit the creative possibilities of radically challenging, dislodging, and transforming the *ideological and in-*

*stitutional premises* of this condition of domestic warfare in favor of short-term, "winnable" policy reforms? (For example, why did we choose to formulate and tolerate a "progressive" political language that *reinforced* dominant racist notions of "criminality" in the process of trying to discredit the legal basis of "Three Strikes" laws?) What were the fundamental concerns of our progressive organizations and movements during this time, and were they willing to comprehend and galvanize an effective, or even viable opposition to the white supremacist state's *terms of engagement* (that is, *warfare*)? This radical accountability reflects a variation on anticolonial liberation theorist Frantz Fanon's memorable statement to his own peers, comrades, and nemeses:

> Each generation must discover its mission, fulfill it or betray it, in relative opacity. In the underdeveloped countries preceding generations have simultaneously resisted the insidious agenda of colonialism and paved the way for the emergence of the current struggles. Now that we are in the heat of combat, we must shed the habit of decrying the efforts of our forefathers or feigning incomprehension at their silence or passiveness.

Lest we fall victim to a certain political nostalgia that is often induced by such illuminating Fanonist exhortations, we ought to clarify the premises of the social "mission" that our generation of US based progressive organizing has undertaken.

In the vicinity of the constantly retrenching social welfare apparatuses of the US state, much of the most urgent and immediate work of community-based organizing has revolved around service provision. Importantly, this pragmatic focus also builds a certain progressive ethic of voluntarism that constructs the model activist as a variation on older liberal notions of the "good citizen." Following Fanon, the question is whether and how this mission ought to be fulfilled or betrayed. I believe that to respond to this political problem requires an analysis and conceptualization of "the state" that is far more complex and laborious than we usually allow in our ordinary rush of obligations to build campaigns, organize communities, and write grant proposals. In fact, I think one pragmatic step toward an abolitionist politics involves the development of grassroots pedagogies (such as reading groups, in-home workshops, inter-organization and inter-movement critical dialogues) that will compel us to teach ourselves about the different ways that the state works in the context of domestic warfare, so that we no longer treat it simplistically. We require, in other words, a *scholarly* activist framework to understand that the state can and must be radically confronted on multiple fronts by *an abolitionist politics*.

In so many ways, the US progressive/left establishment is filling the void created by what Ruthie Gilmore has called the violent "abandonments" of the state, which

forfeits and implodes its own social welfare capacities (which were already insufficient at best) while transforming and (productively) exploding its domestic warmaking functionalities (guided by a "frightening willingness to engage in human
sacrifice"). Yet, at the same time that the state has been openly galvanizing itself to
declare and wage violent struggle against strategically targeted local populations,
the establishment left remains relatively unwilling and therefore institutionally unable to address the questions of social survival, grassroots mobilization, radical social justice, and social transformation *on the concrete and everyday terms of the
very domestic war(s) that the state has so openly and repeatedly declared as the
premises of its own coherence.*

## PITFALLS OF THE PEDAGOGICAL STATE

We can broadly understand that "the state" is in many ways a conceptual term that
refers to a mind-boggling array of geographic, political, and institutional relations
of power and domination. It is, in that sense, a term of abstraction: certainly the
state is "real," but it is so massive and institutionally stretched that it simply cannot be understood and "seen" in its totality. The way we come to comprehend the
state's realness—or differently put, the way the state makes itself comprehensible,
intelligible, and materially identifiable to ordinary people—is through its own self-
narrations and institutional mobilizations.

Consider the narrative and institutional dimensions of the "war on drugs," for
example. New York City mayor Edward Koch, in a gesture of masculine challenge
to the Reagan-era Feds, offers a prime example of such a narration in a 1986 op-ed
piece published on the widely-read pages of *The New York Times*:

I propose the following steps as a coordinated Federal response to [the war
on drugs]:

Use the full resources of the military for drug interdiction. The Posse Comitatus
doctrine, which restricts participation of the military in civilian law enforcement, must be modified so that the military can be used for narcotics control ...

Enact a Federal death penalty for drug wholesalers. Life sentences, harsh fines,
forfeitures of assets, billions spent on education and therapy all have failed to
deter the drug wholesaler. The death penalty would. Capital punishment is an
extraordinary remedy, but we are facing an extraordinary peril ...

Designate United States narcotics prisons. The Bureau of Prisons should designate separate facilities for drug offenders. Segregating such prisoners from

others, preferably in remote locations such as the Yukon or desert areas, might motivate drug offenders to abandon their trade.

Enhance the Federal agencies combating the drug problem. The Attorney General should greatly increase the number of drug enforcement agents in New York and other cities. He should direct the Federal Bureau of Investigation to devote substantial manpower against the cocaine trade and should see to it that the Immigration and Naturalization Service is capable of detecting and deporting aliens convicted of drug crimes in far better numbers than it now does.

Enact the state and local narcotics control assistance act of 1986. This bill provides $750 million annually for five years to assist state and local jurisdictions increase their capacities for enforcement, corrections, education and prosecution.

These proposals offer no certainty for success in the fight against drugs, of course. If we are to succeed, however, it is essential that we persuade the Federal Government to recognize its responsibility to lead the way.

Edward Koch's manifesto reflects an important dimension of the broader institutional, cultural, and political activities that build the state as a mechanism of self-legitimating violence: the state (here momentarily manifest in the person of the New York City Mayor) constantly *tells stories about itself*, facilitated by a politically willing and accomplice corporate media.

This storytelling—which through repetition and saturation assembles the popular "common sense" of domestic warfare—is inseparable from the on-the-ground shifting, rearranging, and recommitting of resources and institutional power that we witness in the everyday mobilizations of a state waging intense, localized, militarized struggle against its declared internal enemies. Consider, for example, how pronouncements like those of Koch, Reagan, and Bratton seem to always be accompanied by the operational innovation of different varieties of covert ops, urban guerilla war, and counterintelligence warfare that specifically emerge through the state's declared domestic wars on crime/drugs/gangs/etc. Hence, it is no coincidence that Mayor Koch's editorial makes the stunning appeal to withdraw ("modify") the Posse Comitatus principle, to allow the Federal government's formal mobilization of its global war apparatus for battle in the homeland neighborhoods of the war on drugs. To reference our example even more closely, we can begin to see how the ramped-up policing and massive imprisonment of Black and Latino youth in Koch's 1980s New York were *enabled and normalized* by his and others' attempts to storytell the legal empowerment and cultural valorization of the police, such that the nuts-and-bolts operation of the prison industrial complex was lubricated by the multiple moral parables of domestic warfare.

This process of producing the state as an active, tangible, and identifiable structure of power and dominance, through the work of self-narration and concrete mobilizations of institutional capacity, is what some scholars call "statecraft." Generally, the state materializes and becomes comprehensible to us through these definitive moments of crafting: that is, we come to identify the state as a series of active political and institutional *projects*. So, if the state's self-narration inundates us with depictions of its policing and juridical arms as the righteously punitive and justifiably violent front lines of an overlapping series of comprehensive, militarized, and culturally valorized domestic wars—for my generation, the "war on drugs," the generation prior, the "war on crime," and the current generation, localized "wars on gangs" and their planetary rearticulation in the "war on terror"—then it is the *material processes of war*, from the writing of public policy to the hyper-weaponization of the police, that commonly represents the existence of the state as we come to normally "know" it.

Given that domestic warfare composes both the common narrative language and concrete material production of the state, the question remains as to why the establishment left has not confronted this statecraft with the degree of absolute emergency that the condition implies (war!). Perhaps it is because we are underestimating the skill and reach of the state as a pedagogical (teaching) apparatus, replete with room for contradiction and relatively sanctioned spaces for "dissent" and counter-state organizing. Italian political prisoner Antonio Gramsci's thoughts on the formation of the contemporary pedagogical state are instructive here:

> The State does have and request consent, but it also "educates" this consent, by means of the political and syndical associations; these, however, are private organisms, left to the private initiative of the ruling class.

Although Gramsci was writing these words in the early 1900s, he had already identified the institutional symbiosis that would eventually produce the non-profit industrial complex. The historical record of the last three decades shows that liberal foundations such as the Ford, Mellon, Rockefeller, Soros and other financial entities have become politically central to "the private initiative of the ruling class" and have in fact funded a breath-taking number of organizations, grassroots campaigns, and progressive political interests. The questions I wish to insert here, however, are whether the financially enabling gestures of foundations also 1) exert a politically disciplinary or repressive force on contemporary social movements and community based organizations, while 2) nurturing an ideological and structural *allegiance to the state* that preempts a more creative, radical, abolitionist politics.

Several social movement scholars have argued that the "channeling mechanisms" of the non-profit industrial complex "may now far outweigh the effect of direct social control by states in explaining the ... orthodox tactics, and moderate goals of much collective action in modern America." The non-profit apparatus and its symbiotic relationship to the state amount to a sophisticated technology of political repression and social control, *accompanying and facilitating the ideological and institutional mobilizations of a domestic war waging state.* Avowedly progressive, radical, leftist, and even some misnamed "revolutionary" groups find it opportune to assimilate into this state-sanctioned organizational paradigm, as it simultaneously allows them to establish a relatively stable financial and operational infrastructure while avoiding the transience, messiness, and possible legal complication of working under decentralized, informal, or even "underground" auspices. Thus, the aforementioned authors suggest that the emergence of the state-proctored non-profit industry "suggests a historical movement away from direct, cruder forms [of state repression], toward more subtle forms of state social control of social movements."

The regularity with which progressive organizations immediately forfeit the crucial political and conceptual possibilities of abolishing domestic warfare is a direct reflection of the extent to which domestic war has been fashioned into the *everyday, "normal" reality of the state.* By extension, the non-profit industrial complex, which is fundamentally guided by the logic of being state-sanctioned (and often state-funded), also reflects this common reality: the operative assumptions of domestic warfare are *taken for granted because they form and inform the popular consensus.*

Effectively contradicting, decentering, and transforming the popular consensus (for example, destabilizing assertive assumptions common to progressive movements and organizations such as "we have to control/get rid of gangs," "we need prisons," or "we want better police") is, in this context, dangerously difficult work. Although, the truth of the matter is that the establishment US left, in ways both spoken and presumed, may actually *agree* with the political, moral, and ideological premises of domestic warfare. Leaders as well as rank-and-file members in avowedly progressive organizations can and must reflect on how they might actually be supporting and reproducing existing forms of racism, white supremacy, state violence, and domestic warfare in the process of throwing their resources behind what they perceive as "winnable victories," in the lexicon of venerable community organizer Saul Alinsky.

Our historical moment suggests the need for a principled political rupturing of existing techniques and strategies that fetishize and fixate on the negotiation, massaging, and management of the worst outcomes of domestic warfare. One political move long overdue is toward grassroots pedagogies of radical *dis-identification* with the state, in the trajectory of an anti-nationalism or anti-patriotism, that reorients a progressive *identification* with the creative possibilities of insurgency (this is to consider "insurgency" as a politics that pushes beyond the defensive maneuvering of "resistance"). Reading a few a few lines down from our first invoking of Fanon's call to collective, liberatory action is clarifying here: "For us who are determined to break the back of colonialism, our historic mission is to authorize every revolt, every desperate act, and every attack aborted or drowned in blood."

While there are rare groups in existence that offer this kind of nourishing political space (from the L.A.-based Youth Justice Coalition to the national organization INCITE! Women of Color Against Violence), they are often forced to expend far too much energy challenging both the parochialisms of the hegemonic non-profit apparatus and the sometimes narrow politics of the progressive US left.

## CONCLUSION: ABOLITION AND RADICAL POLITICAL VISION

I have become somewhat obsessed with amplifying the need for a dramatic, even spectacular political shift that pushes against and reaches beyond the implicit pro-state politics of left progressivism. Most importantly, I am convinced that the abolition of domestic warfare, not unlike precedent (and ongoing) struggles to abolish colonialism, slavery, and programmatic genocide, necessitates a rigorous theoretical and pragmatic approach to a counter- and anti-state radicalism that attempts to fracture the foundations of the existing US social form—because after all, there is truly nothing to be redeemed of a society produced through such terror-inspiring structures of dominance. This political shift requires a sustained labor of radical vision, and in the most crucial ways is actually anchored to "progressive" notions of life, freedom, community, and collective/personal security (including safety from racist policing/criminalization and the most localized brutalities of neoliberal or global capitalism).

Arguably, it is precisely the *creative and pragmatic* work of political fantasy/ political vision/political imagination that is the most underdeveloped dimension of the US establishment left's organizational modus operandi and public discourse. While a full discussion is best left for another essay, we might consider the post-1960s history of the reactionary, neoconservative, and Christian fundamentalist US right, which has fully and eagerly engaged in these political labors of fantasy/vision/imagination, and has seen the desires of their wildest dreams met or exceeded in their struggles for political and cultural hegemony. It might be useful to begin by thinking of ourselves as existing in a relationship of deep historical obligation to the long and recent, faraway and nearby historical legacies of radical, revolutionary, and liberationist struggles that have made the abolition of oppressive violence their most immediate and fundamental political desire.

DYLAN RODRÍGUEZ *is an Associate Professor at University of California-Riverside, where he began his teaching career in 2001. His first book,* Forced Passages: Imprisoned Radical Intellectuals and the US Prison Regime *was published in 2006 by the University of Minnesota Press. Among other political-intellectual collectives, he has worked with and/or alongside such organizations as Critical Resistance, INCITE! (a progressive antiviolence movement led by radical women of color, see incite-national.org), the Critical Filipino and Filipina Studies Collective (cffsc.focusnow.org), and the editorial board of the internationally recognized journal* Social Justice: A Journal of Crime, Conflict, and World Order.

*Reprinted from* Without Fear: Claiming Safe Communities Without Sacrificing Ourselves *edited by the Southern California Library.*

# TOXIC CONNECTIONS: COALITION STRATEGIES AGAINST JAIL EXPANSION

*Damien Domenack and Rachael Leiner*

The Community in Unity coalition (CIU) began its formation when members of Rights for Imprisoned People with Psychiatric Disabilities (RIPPD) learned about a proposal for a 2,000-bed jail at the Oak Point, Hunts Point section of the Bronx from a newspaper article detailing a city council hearing held in April 2006. Prior to the hearing there had been no community outreach or education around the jail proposal, and no notice that the proposal would be presented before the City Council. RIPPD and the Bronx Defenders met with members of Critical Resistance-NYC to talk about the citywide jail expansion plan; the groups then went to a meeting hosted by Sustainable South Bronx (SSB) at the Bronx Defender offices. The Community in Unity coalition meeting made up a large spectrum of the South Bronx community—RIPPD, CR-NYC, For A Better Bronx (FABB), Sustainable South Bronx, Asociación Pro Derechos del Confinado, The Bronx Defenders, the Point Community Development Corporation, Mothers on the Move, Justice Works Community, and the Seven Neighborhood Action Partnership (SNAP). During that meeting, SSB tried to get organizations on board with their "green jobs not jails" campaign, which proposed to build a recycling plant on the site in place of a jail. There were concerns in offering only one alternative, whether or not to make it a site-specific issue (or stand against the jail itself), and in the end no agreements were reached.

From the beginning it was apparent that the struggle against the Oak Point jail was going to be a journey—one that would take all of the organizations and community members involved to look for community solutions to the proposed jail, and also to engage directly with the violence of the prison industrial complex (PIC) and the ways in which these issues impact us everyday.

Some groups first found out about the jail through local newspapers; these delivered the news of a proposal that would directly affect our community right to our door steps, all while public officials avoided open pronouncements about the controversial plan. It was only through the newspapers that people uncovered the decisions being made about our community. Clearly, our elected officials (who are paid with our tax dollars) had not bothered to ask the opinions of the local community that dwells there. It would later come to light that Adolfo Carrion, the Bronx Borough President at the time, made a statement that the jail should be built in the South Bronx because so many members of our community would end up there anyway.

In order to work together to understand the nature of the PIC, the coalition had to come together in the spirit of unity despite our own agendas. We were determined to see that the intended $375 million dollars would be used for something that would support us as a community, and not something that would result in the same racism and violence that has been so common to the South Bronx. Community in Unity came together through this struggle to create alternatives to the proposed jail.

Since the industrial boom, the South Bronx has worn a shifting face and played a shifting role in the economic and social development of New York City. After World War II the demographics changed from mostly working class Irish and Jewish immigrants, to Puerto Rican and African Americans migrating North looking for work and better quality of life. As more people of color came to the South Bronx, it became apparent that the phenomenon of white flight was spurring on an economic downfall. Many of the factories that employed thousands laid off hundreds of workers and some businesses folded all together. With land readily being used for any economic gain, the South Bronx was carved amongst businesses that catered to industrial traffic, and as a result, a huge, disproportionate level of diesel truck traffic flowed through it. So the South Bronx, with four nuclear power plants, a juvenile detention center, a jail barge situated on the docks, Rikers Island (which is housed atop an old landfill), and the country's largest food distribution market and trucking industry, nearly became a political cess pool and a virtual "dumping" ground. Its vibrant community was left to be burned by greedy land lords and abandoned by businesses that turned a blind eye to the nature of the issues that its residents faced. Even now the average household income in the Mott Haven section of the Bronx is less than ten thousand dollars a year according to a 2005 census.

However, the hidden agendas of some groups that later joined the coalition would ultimately reveal larger issues that must be critically looked at when struggling for the emancipation and dignity of our community. It was apparent when CIU first convened that there were organizational entities operating with hidden agendas to push for plans that would use the property for other business ventures, despite the fact that all of the organizations and community members within the coalition had made an agreement to fight solely against the city's plan for jail expansion. These agendas unfolded as the coalition pushed forward with its mission to fight against the jail. It was the call for abolition that rallied organizations and community members to struggle together. Critical Resistance members and organizers played a crucial role in bringing to light what abolition is, and what it means to fight against the PIC as a whole—at its roots of imperialism and violence and not as a broken piece in an otherwise just system.

While organizations involved already had a clear understanding of the flaws of society, and many of them state within their missions to seek justice for their communities along similar lines, abolition was a crucial means of unfolding our understanding of an imperialist system and unifying us further in this struggle to fight against Commissioner Horn and the Department of Corrections (DOC). As the coalition moved forward with its understanding of abolition, some of the organizational partners began to move further outside of the core of the coalition and used the hard work of organizations like Critical Resistance, RIPPD, Seven Neighborhood Action Partnership, For A Better Bronx, Mothers on the Move, and Sistas on the Rise as a catapult to build another facility similar to the ones that currently bring large amounts of pollution (because of their intended use) and traffic into the community.

In addition, some of these organizations started campaigns that are new and emerging around the country, focusing on "green jobs and not jails" as their platforms. Several CR members and organizers were approached to join this campaign. While the slogan sounded good, the reality is that jobs in these facilities would expose low-income and working class people to toxics—contributing to already existing health problems and developing new environmental health problems. As issues were raised inside of the collective, the coalition saw the dwindling numbers of its active membership as an indication of where the organizations that were calling for "green jobs, not jails" were coming from; the way information was shared, and how these organizations benefited from community based movements to further their agendas created tension. Even though, internal conflicts within the coalition peaked and the burn of these conflicts pushed activists to hold open conversations that also resulted in the loss of active members; however, as a result, the issue of hidden agendas was blown wide open.

As the seasons changed, the battle raged on and people took to the streets to let the community know what they thought of the proposed jail. The coalition worked fiercely to develop 50 alternatives to the jail at Oak Point, and organized outreach to community members to attend meetings and hearings being held by the Department of Corrections. Women from La Casita (a residential substance abuse treatment facility for mothers with children and mothers to be) organized and attended a public hearing with protest signs in hand in order to have their voices heard and bring their experiences to the forefront regarding the decision to use $375 million dollars to build a new jail. They stressed that health insurance, jobs, childcare, good education, and support services were needed. Their presence at that gathering was extremely impactful as women that are currently experiencing the violent effects of the PIC on their lives and the lives of their families.

In the spring of 2008, it seemed as though the combined efforts of CIU had reached its pinnacle; the Department of Corrections began to circulate a statement that the proposed jail site was not going to work and that their plans to place the jail at the Oak Point, Hunts Point land was not going to happen. At first, coalition members didn't believe the rumors, and tried to dig up as much information from reliable sources to verify the story prior to celebrating.

Although it was true, the Department of Corrections was not able to secure the Oak Point site, which meant that in essence the plans for the jail had been defeated, activists and organizers still felt weary about the situation. There was brief rejoicing until, weeks later, the DOC unveiled their plans to locate the jail on a piece of property that they were in current possession of. The battle was once again ignited!

Now the Department of Corrections was wise to the strategy of CIU, activists, organizers, and community members. They began to strategize ways to combat the efforts of the coalition by appealing to individual organizations that functioned as a part of the coalition. When Commissioner Martin Horn tried this tactic, believing that recent strife in the past had weakened communication and solidarity between organizations, he found that opposition was stronger than he had anticipated. Coalition members from The Point Community Development Corporation put out an email about an invitation to speak with Commissioner Horn in private, and Mothers on the Move (MOMs) also received a similar notice. MOMs however decided to open their private meeting up to the community to expose the underhandedness of Commissioner Horn to carry over his plans by making closed door deals, and hoping that organizations, organizers, and activists would betray the spirit of abolition and sell out our brothers and sisters! The nerve!

Coalition members and community members filled the small offices of MOMs to let Commissioner Horn know that their stance in opposition to the jail still stood and that they could not be swayed by behind-the-scenes deals and back-door promises. Some of what the Department of Corrections was offering were community solutions to other issues that organizations, activists, and community members had been struggling to attain for decades. The DOC wasn't even coming to the table with their own ideas, but ideas that they had gotten from the community! Nevertheless, CR organizers spoke to Commissioner Horn, stating that as long as there was a PIC, we would stand against it—in order to stop the criminalization of our communities, our neighborhoods, and our youth—to stop policies that underestimate our demands for something better for our communities.

Still, the struggle continues and our campaign has geared up for the summer of 2008, CIU stands strong and united despite the always pending violence of the PIC. It is the spirit of abolition that continues to remind participants, and inform community members of why struggling against the PIC is about seeking community solutions to imprisonment, imperialism, racism, environmental racism, sexism, homophobia, transphobia, heterosexism, poverty, hunger, homelessness, discrimination, and addiction—these are the by-products of an unjust system.

**DAMIEN DOMENACK,** *of Critical Resistance New York City, is a twenty-seven-year-old, Latino parent who lives in the South Bronx with his family. Damien began organizing in 2004 with TransJustice, a trans and gender non-conforming people of color collective that fights for the basic human rights and freedom for all people. He has proven how committed and dedicated he is to the people of the Trans and gender-non conforming and other South Bronx communities that face the daily struggles of survival.*

**RACHAEL LEINER** *is a twenty-seven-year-old, native-born Bronxite and New Yorker and an active member in the CR-NYC chapter. Rachael supports the efforts for the La Casita project and recently joined CR staff to continue to keep the presence of abolition, organizing, and resistance with the women of the La Casita program. Rachael currently supports environmental justice efforts in the South Bronx working in community gardens with gardeners, youth, and community members in an effort to reclaim space, grow food, support spaces of community based education, intergenerational connection, radical politics, and family.*

# PRICKLY COALITIONS: MOVING PRISON ABOLITIONISM FORWARD

*Alexander Lee*

Transgender and gender variant people have a lot to gain from the abolition of the prison industrial complex (PIC), yet these communities currently have no choice but to rely on law enforcement for at least the appearance of protection from the daily threat of physical assault and murder. But as with other communities severely negatively impacted by the PIC and also forced to rely upon it, the root causes of this contradiction give us insight into what we must do to build a world that no longer needs cages and prisons as "cure-alls" for social ills.

Regional surveys and anecdotal evidence suggest that transgender and gender variant people (and especially trans and gender variant people of color) are grossly overrepresented in our nation's prisons and jails. In the San Francisco Bay Area, with a population of over 20,000 transgender people, close to 1 in 2 transgender people have been in prison or jail. These rates of imprisonment are actually not surprising—with astronomically high poverty and unemployment rates, most transgender and gender variant people have had to resort to "survival crime" just to put food on the table. Furthermore, some of the most extreme incidents of transphobic hate violence and harassment occur within prison walls—abuse that is approved without question or openly committed by state and federal governments.

Trans and gender variant people imprisoned in the PIC are denied all forms of self-determination on the basis of identity and expression. Legal name and gender marker changes are voided, physical genitalia is the deciding factor, transition-related health care is non-existent in most jurisdictions, and physical, sexual, and psychological torture is the norm. Just as prison administrators manipulate and heighten tensions among racial groups by pitting racial gangs against each other, they reinforce rigid gender roles through discriminatory policies and rape that effectively place transgender and gender variant people at the bottom of prison social hierarchies.

As most transgender and gender variant people in prison are eventually released, they return to communities so weakened by discrimination that they are unable to access the social and healthcare services needed to heal from these traumatic experiences, and to find legal means to generate income—thereby setting the stage for the revolving door of imprisonment and the street. The PIC is very much a plague upon our communities, and its destructive role in all our lives must be addressed if we are ever to reach full liberation.

At the same time, transgender and gender variant people in the "free world," especially those on the male-to-female spectrum who are low-income and of color, live on the razor's edge. Every day is a precarious balance between passing (life) and being unwillingly "clocked" (death). Transgender teenager Gwen Araujo's much-publicized murder by other youths is only the tip of the iceberg; the website "Remembering Our Dead" (http://www.gender.org/remember) keeps a running count of transgender and transsexual people murdered, sometimes by police, around the country. Most people have never heard of the people on this list (the publicity following Gwen's death was very much an aberration), but each of their deaths, and the years of hustling against racism, poverty, sexism, and the gender binary system that preceded these tragic ends, reverberates profoundly in the bones of every transgender and gender variant person still hustling today.

The reality of ever-present danger forces many transgender and gender variant people, some themselves survivors of anti-transgender hate violence from law enforcement, to rely on the prison industrial complex when they feel their lives are being threatened. But when one decodes, for example, the aggressively pro-death penalty rhetoric from many transgender people and organizations following Gwen's murder, what one really finds is a deep frustration and outrage against the rest of society's assumptions that our communities' right to safety is not legitimate, that our lives have no more worth than a piece of trash on the sidewalk. These assumptions aren't just reinforced by the quiet indifference from larger society when yet another "unidentified man dressed as a woman" is found murdered, but through pervasive anti-transgender (and racist, sexist, classist, etc.) discrimination that prevents us from having stable housing, from landing meaningful jobs, from having access to any kind of health care, from pursuing our educational goals, and from being treated with basic human dignity when we walk down the street.

These are, of course, the same wants and needs of any other oppressed group, and one in the same for transgender people who are also of color, women, immigrants, people with felony convictions, disabled, homeless, etc. These wants and needs are what oppressed communities all over the world need to feel safe, to feel whole, and to end physical, psychological, sexual, and economic violence against us.

How can these needs help shape a strong prison abolition movement? First, we should understand that "prison abolition" means much more than closing down prisons. Instead, the absence of prisons is only one way of describing a society free of systems of inequity—white supremacy, male supremacy and the gender binary, capitalism, ableism, among other things—which produce violence, desperation, hatred, and suffering. Such a society would laugh off the outrageous idea of putting people into cages, thinking such actions as morally perverse and fatally counterproductive. Thus, "abolishing prisons" really means the creation of a society where systemic and historical oppression are wiped out so that everyone's basic needs are met, where child abuse and domestic violence are zeroed out, and where war is absolutely not an option to "protect" ourselves or to drain capital from abroad to inflate a declining domestic economy.

Ironically, the current prison abolition movement is neither the best-suited nor strategically placed to create such a world. This is because the prison abolition movement is currently mostly being pushed forward by people like me—activists (whether they be prisoners, former prisoners, family members of prisoners, lawyers, students—paid or unpaid) who are primarily preoccupied with changing the way people are treated inside prisons, and preventing prison expansion. But if prison abolition requires creating a world where prisons are no longer needed, then the real work of abolition must be done away from prisons—in shelters, health clinics, schools, and in battles over government budget allocations. Prisons and the human rights violations that occur within them are merely distractions from the real problems sustaining their existence.

However, the sectors of society that are mobilizing to meet people's basic needs outside of prisons are by and large not doing their work with the understanding that they too can be prison abolitionists. Most people working in these areas collaborate with law enforcement, both because of the lack of any other adequate options, or because government funding or "mandated reporter" laws require them to do so. Some of them would even consider themselves parts of the political right, like churches that operate soup kitchens and Christian missionary groups building houses for homeless people. Regardless of ideological orientation however, the vast majority of these services are off-limits to transgender and gender variant people anyway because of anti-transgender and homophobic discrimination and prejudice.

Yet because services that provide housing, healthcare and other essentials are the basis from which a world without prisons will be made possible, this is where the prison abolition movement must go next. We must break down funder-created boundaries and ideological barriers between anti-prison activists and service providers, and challenge each other to eliminate our internalized prejudice that prevents everyone from having their basic needs met, and their souls from being satisfied and liberated. As we go forward in this direction, we should expect to be forced to discard language that limits this movement to prisons and the prison industrial complex, in favor of descriptors that foster "prickly coalitions" with others who don't see themselves as anti-prison, but who do believe in the sacred nature of human dignity, however imperfectly expressed in practice. This new language and these new alliances will and should transcend party lines and the same old tired political rhetoric. Thus, we may have to stop calling ourselves "prison abolitionists" in favor of new alliances that reflect the truly wide-ranging scope of our aspirations.

The prison abolition movement must expand its arms to envelope the same people who fight for housing but demonize prisoners, who protest war but love to watch "CSI," people who march for civil rights but yell "maricón!" at trans-women, and queers who demand the death penalty when yet another one of us is murdered. We should move into these other sectors and act as the lodestar pulling everyone towards the ultimate goal of building a world where liberation is the status quo. When we achieve these goals, the abolition of prisons will just be the icing on the cake.

ALEXANDER L. LEE *is the founder and Director of the Transgender, Gender Variant & Intersex Justice Project (TGIJP), a nonprofit legal advocacy and community organizing center in San Francisco. TGIJP is the only organization dedicated full-time to providing legal services and community organizing assistance to transgender persons experiencing human rights violations in California prisons.*

*This article was originally published in Critical Resistance's* The Abolitionist *(Issue 4).*

# CAN YOU UNDERSTAND?

*Souligma Phothong*

I refuse to accuse this result
As being the product of indifference from society
No fault lies in the possession of my father
My mother blessed me
With all the virtues that are apparent
In my essence today
I labor under the burden
Of accepting responsibility
For my late transgressions
I make no excuses
I am a man

All I want is for you to understand

Dearest Mama
Please do not be afraid
Independence means you are
No longer subjected to his abuse
Not that you are alone
Sister and I, will help you
Raise us
I am so fortunate
That you do not comprehend fully

The ways of this foreign world
That your love
Impairs your sight
Of the biased perception you have
Of me
For nothing else in existence
Could hide the adulterated butterfly
I have become
Your graceful presence
For an eternity
Will be mourned
Thank you celestial Father
For closing her eyes
Before she could witness
What has befallen her child

She would not understand

Dearest Papa
I am proud of you
For slaying the monster
That manifested itself
Through your indelible
Atrocities
If you did not leave
Redemption could not be achieved
Relieve yourself
Of the regret
That is so evident in your eyes
This is something I had to endure
Were it not for this
How else could I be
The serene spirit that
I am today
I wandered along the rugged
Edge of the cliff
And stumbled
But my fist is firmly clenched

On the branch of enlightenment
I will rise!
And no longer wallow
In the pungent decay of this cycle
Generations ago
After disrespecting myself
By mistreating you
You lovingly prophesied that
Although at present I fail to understand
One day
A coup
Will precipitate
A revolution within my being

I finally understand

Dear Mr. Governor
I was rebellious and impressionable
Allowing these defective traits in humanity
To overwhelm my compassion
Consequently
The judge decided against throwing away the key
He entrusted it to you
Love, patience, and acceptance
Has already set me free
It is now time
For you to be released
For the duration of my life
The souls that were sacrificed
Cannot be resurrected
In their place
Is scar tissue
Inside the hearts of loved ones
And the deprivation
That has enhanced
My character
I plead for your empathy
I am not worthy of your sympathy

Shatter these chains
That constrict the breath of my family
It is getting late
Please do not keep my mother awake
Waiting
With tears flooding her grave
Allow her tortured specter to rest
Allow me to come home
I have found the path
This pen is my heart
I am bleeding these words out to you

Can you understand?

SOULIGMA PHOTHONG *is the Laotian son of two parents whose love was so un-selfish, he is incapable of defining ... Love.*

*Reprinted from* Other: an Asian & Pacific Islander Prisoners' Anthology, *with permission from the Asian Prisoner Support Committee (APSC).* Other *is the first book to highlight the unique stories and perspectives of the growing Asian prisoner population in the US It is available now on Amazon.com.*

# SECTION 3:
# BUILD

# CARCERAL LANDSCAPE IN HAWAI'I:
# THE POLITICS OF EMPIRE,
# THE COMMODIFICATION OF BODIES,
# AND A WAY HOME

*RaeDeen Keahiolalo-Karasuda*

## INTRODUCTION

Across the globe, Hawai'i is described as one of the most idyllic places on earth. Advertised as a virtual paradise, more than 7 million visitors flock to the Hawaiian archipelago each year for pleasure and relaxation (Trask 1999, 1993). But the actual history of Hawai'i and her people contradicts those pictures of perfection sold and distributed throughout the world. Since the mid-1970s, imprisonment rates on the US continent quadrupled (Travis and Waul 2003). During the same time, the prison population in Hawai'i increased fifteen-fold, which included a 700% increase in the Hawaiian prisoner population—far outstripping the general Hawaiian population growth, which increased by about 300% over the same period (Keahiolalo-Karasuda 2007). According to the State of Hawai'i's Department of Public Safety, Hawaiians represent 20% percent of Hawai'i's general population, but comprise 40% percent of the state's imprisoned population (State of Hawai'i Department of Public Safety (DPS) 2003).[1] Firsthand accounts of prisoners, families, advocates, and prison industrial complex professionals, however, suggest that Hawaiians actually represent more than 60% of imprisoned people in the state.

---

1   *Kanaka Maoli, Hawaiian,* and *Kanaka 'Ōiwi* are interchangeably used to describe Hawai'i's first peoples. *State of Hawai'i* and *state* is used to reference the current neocolonial government which continues to illegally occupy the Hawaiian archipelago.

In the early 1990s, sociologist Gene Kassebaum, found that Hawaiians were imprisoned at twice the rate of their representation in the general population, while East Asians who were 31.9% of the general populace made up 5.3% of the prison population, and whites, 29.8% of Hawai'i's residents at that time, were less than 23% of those sentenced to prison. (Kassebaum 1994) Kassebaum likewise notes that Hawaiians were often convicted for "property-related offenses," and "minor probation and parole violations" (Ibid: 5). He writes,

> The data show that the risk of being sanctioned by state or county agencies, of being removed from home, job and community for either short or long periods of time, or acquiring a criminal record and jail or prison experience, continues to be a burden on the Hawaiian community. That risk climbs as the defining event moves from arrest to prosecution to judgment and sentencing ... [T]here are too many Hawaiians in prison (Ibid: 7-3).

Clearly, the deeper Kanaka Maoli are pressed into the prison industrial complex, via policing and surveillance the more likely they are to be sent to prison.

Although many scholars and popular writers have produced work about the colonization of Hawai'i, their treatments have neglected the subject of carceral politics. When I speak about carceral politics or the colonial carceral, I am expanding on Foucault's definition of the carceral network: "The carceral network, in its compact or disseminated forms, with its systems of insertion, distribution, surveillance, observation has been the greatest support, in modern society, of the normalizing of power" (Foucault 1977). Hence, carceral politics and the prison industrial complex is/are steeped in imperialist and colonialist traditions, where the imprisonment of Hawaiians and the carceral archipelago as a site of disposal has become so normalized that it operates without any real debate or intervention. Using an interdisciplinary approach, I piece together a portrait of the colonial carceral, demonstrating that, for over one hundred years, colonizers have deployed drug wars and imprisonment as mechanisms of colonization against Kanaka 'Ōiwi.

How has the prison industrial complex impacted the lives of Hawaiians over time? I begin by discussing the deployment of the 19th century War on Opium against Hawai'i's last ruling monarch, Queen Lili'uokalani, to illegally dethrone her and take her nation captive. By analyzing the role of the opium war in the colonial project, I demonstrate the importance of reversing the colonial gaze to dismantle the prison industrial complex. This reversal reveals colonial agendas, not disenfranchised individuals and groups, as harmful and violent. Then I provide a brief overview of current state policies which banish Kanaka 'Ōiwi to private, for-profit punishment warehouses more than 3,000 miles away from their homeland. I show how exiling Hawaiians not only separates them from lands and politics, but virtually strips them of any physical contact with family and community. In the ever-expanding prison industrial complex (Davis 2003; Gilmore 2002; Hallett 2004), I question the fact that roughly half of Hawai'i's prisoners (disproportionately Hawaiians) are shipped to US private for-profit prison warehouses owned by Corrections Corporation of America (CCA). The forced removal from homeland— sometimes for years and sometimes for life—is exacerbated by the fact that the State of Hawai'i recently contracted with CCA to build a private prison especially for the purpose of consolidating Hawaiian bodies, making the state among CCA's top list of clients (Dayton September 29, 2006; Talvi 2006).

Lastly, I describe my project as a 2007 Open Society Institute Soros Justice Fellow. Ninety-five percent of people imprisoned will return to community. Prisoners, activists, scholars and practitioners are rightly concerned about advancing effective paths of support for those who are reentering general society. The basic tenets of reentry, including increased and improved health, employment, education, housing and other important opportunities are crucial. But the systemic dismantling of the prison industrial complex is equally important. Hawaiians have been historically criminalized through structural colonialism; thus, deconstructing imprisonment must occur through anti-hegemonic solutions as well. I discuss one way from which to consider what I call, *political reintegration.*

## OVERTHROWING THE HAWAIIAN NATION:
## THE 19TH CENTURY OPIUM WAR

Scholarly studies about colonialism in Hawai'i demonstrate the methods by which power and dominance operate (Kauanui 2002; Osorio 2002; Liliuokalani 1990; Trask 1999; Silva 2004; Kame'eleihiwa 1992). Yet scholars and others have overlooked the role of the prison industrial complex in the illegal overthrow of the Hawaiian kingdom. Likewise, current attention to the study of drugs and crime generally concentrates on individual or group determinants rather than institutionalized violence. This is misleading, especially since the colonization of Hawai'i is directly traceable to the 19th century War on Opium and current practices of punishment. State and popularized efforts to eradicate "social problems" related to drugs in Hawai'i tend to target individual or group problems and rest on the proposition that Hawaiians are prone to addiction and crime. (Hishinuma 2005). Explanations for (actual or perceived) drug-related behaviors are contextualized as responses to historical and cultural trauma (Cook, Withy, and Tarallo-Jensen 2003) or as reactions to economic poverty (Kana'iaupuni, Malone, and Ishibashi 2005). All of these explanations fail to uncover and account for the impacts of systemic and institutional violence. Thus, "experts" condition the public to believe that Hawaiians are prone to addiction and crime or that their behaviors are *because of* historical distress—in other words, "criminal deviance" among Hawaiians is accepted as the norm.

The lack of political discussion directs attention away from the uses of state power against Hawaiians while naturalizing the logic that Hawaiians require a high level of state intervention because of their character deficiencies. The excessive study of Hawaiian criminality also depoliticizes this population and justifies policies that exert stringent social control.

In this essay, I reject the focus on individualized misconduct of a depoliticized people and instead analyze the prison industrial complex in the context of imperial and colonial expansion. I am interested in de-mythologizing the idea of the (taken-for-granted) native criminal and in raising questions about even well-meaning re-entry approaches and the ways in which therapeutic intervention might contribute to keeping the revolving door of prison moving in the same direction. Continuing to associate "psychoactive substance use … as an indicator of some inherent deficiency" (Adrian 2002: 862) in disenfranchised societies must be assessed alongside obvious policies of punishment and colonization.

What role did the US War on Drugs play in the illegal overthrow of Queen Lili'uokalani and her country in 1893? How did colonial conspirators use the opium scare to justify the colonization of Hawai'i? After decades of attempting to usurp monarchical power, a gang of thirteen colonial deviants with the aid of US soldiers from the U.S.S. Boston and US Minister John L. Stevens set their plan in motion on January 16, 1893 to dethrone the queen and take over the Hawaiian archipelago. Soldiers from the U.S.S. Boston landed, marched with rifles through the streets of Honolulu, and stood in plain view fronting the gates of the 'Iolani Palace. On January 17, 1893, standing in formation, marines advanced to the main entrance and aimed their firearms directly at the Palace. Clearly, the United States government was there to back the overthrow of Hawai'i's last ruling monarch. Threatened with bloodshed and loss of life, the queen was forced to abdicate. In order to justify their violence, the usurpers brought three charges against Lili'uokalani. They accused her of attempting to overturn the constitution which they had forced the previous monarch to sign at gunpoint. They charged that the Queen had been considering a lottery bill. And they alleged she was conspiring with the opium trade (Liliuokalani 1990). I discuss the charge in regards to opium. Curtis Marez (2004: x) tells us,

Historically, drug traffic has fueled imperial expansion and global capitalism ...
As a privileged target of police power, drug traffic has also helped to support
and extend the authority of nation-states ... thus suggesting the extent to which
state-sponsored drug wars have brought the ideological and affective intensities
of military power to bear upon the intimate details of everyday life.

By the time colonialists advanced the War on Drugs against Queen Liliʻuokalani,
they had already established a pattern of fear and confusion, spreading false tales
of dangerous natives and impending threats to public safety (Merry 2000; Allen
1994; Brown 2003). Rooted in rumor about the previous monarch, King Kalākaua,
these connections between opium scandals, monarchical ineptitude, and American
security were already in place, available for political uses at a moment's notice. In
1893, the colonialists well understood how opium had been used against the previous monarch to justify colonial revolt and pave the way for the forced signing of the
Bayonet Constitution at gunpoint (Liliuokalani 1990). Now they drew from their
arsenal of drug war rhetoric and deployed this discourse against the queen.

Liliʻuokalani was well aware "prominent citizens" were involved in opium traffic. She worried about this situation, noting at the time,

> Some of the most prominent citizens have been connected with these affairs,
> and frauds have been unearthed even in the custom-house itself ... Mr. Parks, of
> Mr. W.F. Allen, and more recently of Mr. Henry Waterhouse, have been associ-
> ated with some very questionable dealings in this drug; and it may be doubted
> whether the practice of hushing up such matters is favorable to good morals in
> any community. The Provisional Government seems to have had no scruples in
> the matter; for the sons of missionaries exported a large quantity of confiscated
> opium, and sold it for fifty thousand dollars in British Columbia (Liliuokalani
> 1990: 241).

Apparently, the sons of missionaries—"prominent citizens"—stood to lose major profits from the sale of confiscated narcotics and as a result launched a moral
drug crusade. By injecting racialized tales into society about the dangers of opium, colonial druglords were able to "justify revolt against authority, and the sum-
moning of aid of a foreign vessel of war, as they outrageously stated at the time, 'to
protect American life and property!'" (Liliuokalani 1990: 242). Rumor-based
hysteria among foreign residents, along with convoluted tales of monarchical
misdeed diverted attention from the war crimes of imperial expansionists by
framing drugs and crime as a Hawaiian problem. Eclipsing the white face of drug-
dealing, by instituting a brown, native face, the so-called Committee of Public

Safety, with the aid of the US military, set in motion its long-standing plan to steal Hawaiian lands and governance.[2]

The long and arduous struggle of Hawaiians against foreign dominance had taken its toll. Untold waves of cultural, social and political genocide caused tremendous suffering for Lili'uokalani and her people (Allen 1982; Trask 1999; Liliuokalani 1990). Despite their resilience, Hawaiians would face another blow almost two years to the day after the illegal overthrow. On January 16, 1895, Lili'uokalani was arrested and taken into custody ten days after royalists attempted to restore the integrity of their country (Towse 1895; Liliuokalani 1990). Colonial agents, who had the queen and her supporters under constant surveillance, frustrated this attempt, and hundreds were imprisoned. Not surprisingly, colonialists claimed the event was an unprovoked "rebellion" and a threat to the lives of American citizens. Royalists, on the other hand, explained the effort as an act of restorative justice. Colonial gang members pulled out all the stops by rounding up kingdom citizens, throwing them into prison, and stamping the carceral directly into their lives. Lili'uokalani was brought to a swift trial under military tribunal, given no time to prepare her case. She was found guilty of misprision of treason and sentenced to five years hard labor and a $5,000 fine. The colonial Republic forced the queen to abdicate her throne by threatening to execute her supporters if she did not sign the document of abdication. Under extreme duress, she signed; her sentence was then commuted to eight months of imprisonment (Liliuokalani 1990; Allen 1982).

Upon release, Lili'uokalani recalled the feeling of stigma that she carried with her. At a New England reception held in her honor she says,

> The feelings of one who has been imprisoned, politically or otherwise, can only be understood by a person who has passed through the ordeal … it is not easy for me to get over that shrinking from the gaze of strangers acquired by recent years of retirement, eight months of experience as a prisoner, and the humiliations of the time when I was under the supervision of government spies or custodians (Liliuokalani 1990: 317).

Lili'uokalani's statement defines the toll of the colonial prison gaze on the human soul. In spite of her dignity, innocence, and royalty, she felt ashamed beyond the days of physical captivity. Implicating the colonial/carceral gaze, Lili'uokalani gives us insight into the long-lasting impact of carceral brutality.

---

2     Queen Lili'uokalani was considering legislation to license opium. She understood that decriminalizing the drug would enable the government to decrease its punitive practices.

Upon her return home, kingdom citizens showered their queen with adoration and gifts (Irwin 1960). Ten days later on August 12, 1898, the Republic completed its colonial mission. On the steps of 'Iolani Palace, foreign annexationists lowered the kingdom flag and replaced it with red, white, and blue—the so-called American symbol of justice, innocence, and valor.[3] Lili'uokalani dedicated the remainder of her life to redressing the injustices committed against her and her nation (see *Lili'uokalani v. The United States 1910*).

Anthropologist Sally Merry (2002: 417–418) notes that "the creation of a 'criminal' population is a social process that depends on the way offenses are defined, public opinion is excited, and judicial attention is focused … [P]ublic and judiciary interest respond to social reform efforts and economic needs." Merry's observation helps us understand Lili'uokalani and her supporters' attempt to restore their stolen nation; similar patterns exist in tandem with the birth of the modern Hawaiian sovereignty movement which dates back to the 1970s (Trask 1999). In 1972, one woman was imprisoned in Hawai'i. In 1982, there were forty-three—a 4,200% increase in just ten years. From 1992 to 2000, the number of imprisoned women increased from 164 to 500—a 205% increase in just eight years in comparison to a 106% increase on the US continent during the same period. Between 1982 and 2000, women's imprisonment in Hawai'i increased 1,063%. Today, Hawaiian women represent more than half of the statewide imprisoned population. The media is an important source and stimulus of vilification. Leaders in the sovereignty movement are Hawaiian women and are vilified in the press (Keahiolalo-Karasuda 2007), and generally, the media engages in depicting Hawaiians as criminal savages. Analyzing the reality television series *Dog the Bounty Hunter*, Karasuda and Irwin write,

> More than 100 years [after the trumped-up opium charges that facilitated the end of the monarchy], we have a new moral panic, one that is focused on fears of crime. Now criminal justice agents and this reality TV show tell us that the key to public safety is to incarcerate Native Hawaiians—at a rate double that of any other ethnic group in the state. The irony? Public safety equals the criminalization and imprisonment of Native Hawaiians who are severed from their culture. It is important to note that this profit comes at a huge cost to the Native Hawaiian community. The real key to public safety is rehabilitation, including drug treatment, community-based transition programs, and education and employment training—not Dog or punitive crime legislation (Karasuda and Irwin 2005, September 5).

---

3   See www.usflag.org

Representing Kanaka Maoli as poor, drug-addicted, and uncivilized continues to be synonymous with depoliticization and displacement—and prison.

## MARKETING HAWAIIAN BODIES IN THE PRISON INDUSTRIAL COMPLEX

In December 1995, the State of Hawai'i sent its first shipment of 300 men from Hālawa Correctional Facility to two private prisons in Texas (Cunningham n.d.; Dayton 2005).[4] Citing a 1985 consent decree, the state rationalized its decision by invoking the rhetoric of prison overcrowding.[5] Under the current Republican administration, more people than ever have been shipped to foreign punishment centers, allegedly to relieve overcrowding and more recently, as a way of promoting "rehabilitation."

Since 1995, however, prisoners, families, advocates, and ex-CCA staff have filed numerous official and unofficial allegations of contract violations including lack of rehabilitative services, physical and sexual abuse, lack of medical care, and deaths (Dayton 2001; June 2006; 2007). Yet, the state has chosen to turn its back. For example, when 43-year-old Sarah Ah Mau died in December 2005 while at a CCA prison, public safety officials denied that her death had anything to do with her untreated medical complaints of stomach pain for two months prior to her death (Dayton June 2006). In the face of such concerns, the state continues to refuse public accountability (Frank March 31, 2008), and instead partnered with CCA to construct a special $95 million prison especially for the purpose of warehousing prisoners from Hawai'i in Arizona (Dayton June 2006).

How did Hawaiians become a commodity in the prison industrial complex? The practice dates at least as far back as 1976 (*Olim v. Wakinekona*, 461 U.S. 238; 103 S. Ct. 1741; 75 L. Ed. 2d 813 1983) and in fact, the case is part of the seminal legal literature regarding interjurisdictional transfers of prisoners. On August 2, 1976, in response to Delbert Ka'ahanui Wakinekona's advocacy for better prison conditions, prison industrial complex employees at Hālawa Correctional Facility labeled him a "troublemaker" and retaliated against Wakinekona for his outspoken politics (Ibid). They convened a hearing to determine the "reason for which the programs at the maximum control unit of the Hawaii State Prison had failed" and "his program designation at the Hawaii State Prison, which included a possible transfer to an out-

---

4    The Cunningham document is undated and can be retrieved at http://www.doc.state.ok.us/field/
private_prisons/Cross%20Continental%20Cross%20Cultural%20Cooperation%208-13-03.pdf.

5    See *Spear v. Cayetano*

of-state penal facility" (*Wakinekona v. Olim,* 459 F. Supp. 473; 1978 U.S. Dist. LEXIS 17304 1978). Attempting to silence him and justify their retaliatory transfer, the committee reclassified Wakinekona to a higher custody level and banished him to Folsom Penitentiary in California.

After being exiled, Wakinekona filed suit in District Court, citing due process violations (Ibid). The court ruled against Wakinekona, but the 9th Circuit Court of Appeals reversed, deciding that the state created a an interest in liberty from state deprivation of freedom by "promulgating the rule in question and reasoning that the rule gave prisoners a justifiable expectation that they would not be transferred to the mainland absent a hearing, before an impartial committee, concerning the facts alleged in the prehearing notice" (*Wakinekona v. Olim, 664 F.2d 708; 1981 U.S. App. LEXIS 12948 1981*). On appeal, the US Supreme Court ruled that Wakinekona was not deprived of his due process rights, because "prison regulations placed no substantive limitations on official discretion and thus created no liberty interest entitled to protection under the due process" (Olim v. Wakinekona, 461 U.S. 238; 103 S. Ct. 1741; 75 L. Ed. 2d 813 1983). Dissenting Justices Marshall, Brennan, and Stevens wrote that liberty interests were "not limited to whatever a state chooses to bestow" and that "Hawai'i's prison regulations created a liberty interest" (ibid).

The US Supreme Court's sanction in this case of interstate transfers has remained foundational for proponents of privatized punishment. What is lost, however, in a simple account of the court's decision is prison officials' motive for exiling Wakinekona, a man who had been asking for "a special grand jury to investigate conditions at the prison" (Star-Bulletin Staff May 5, 1975). Here, we must consider state exportation as retaliatory banishment and part of the neocolonial agenda to depoliticize and dispossess Kanaka Maoli,

Outsourcing Hawaiian bodies to carceral complexes on the US continent has profound social, cultural, and political consequences for Hawaiians in both past and present. The practice of relegating Hawaiians to a status of *out of sight, out of mind* also has serious implications for the future. As one generation wastes away in prison, another is being dispersed throughout the United States. Compounding the effects of high rates of Hawaiian imprisonment and banishment, the state's foster care system now burgeons with Hawaiian children. Reports indicate 53% of children in foster care are Hawaiian—and the number is climbing (Vorsino 2005, July 11). Prisoners and community members report that there is a growing practice of adopting these children to out-of-state families. Under the guise of off-setting prison overcrowding and providing so-called cost-effective rehabilitation services and reentry possibilities, the steady flow of supply and demand between the state and CCA continues.

## THE POLITICAL REINTEGRATION OF KANAKA MAOLI

The criminalization of Hawaiians is traceable to colonial agendas of disenfranchisement, dispossession, and separation from the political landscape. Likewise, policies of punishment construct ideologies about rehabilitation, where the focus remains on repairing individual deficiencies and group flaws, an orientation that guarantees inadequate and inappropriate "reentry strategies." As a fellow with the Open Society Institute's Soros Justice Fellowship, I am working on a project that places the idea of *political reintegration* at the center of reentry policies, practices, and experiences. The project involves three major components: pilot and develop a cultural politics curriculum, introduce the curriculum and concept to various stakeholders, and produce scholarship to inform others about the potential for a politics-based focus within reentry practices. For the remainder of this essay, I will describe, the pilot classes scheduled August to December 2007, for women residing at a work furlough program. One of my main objectives was to create an intellectually stimulating and interactive learning space where students would be encouraged to participate at a level of their choosing. Students could also have the opportunity to make connections between the content and their personal lives. I developed the lessons by drawing from multiple disciplines, including political science, history and culture, sociology, and journalism.

At first I had planned for twelve two-hour classes geared toward cultural identity, but after discussions with colleagues and more thought, I shifted my attention toward a syllabus that would focus on cultural politics, which encompassed cultural literacy and political activism. The shift was implemented because of my determination that reentry policies must embody and expand political and structural answers to be effective. Early on, I realized it was critical to let the curriculum develop through the experiences of the students and instructor, and not depend on a pre-packaged set of course materials. This approach required much more creativity and flexibility on my part (more than I thought I had). But placing the students' interests and experiences at the heart of the course proved so successful that I increased the number of classes from twelve to twenty-two, and from two hours to six hours each.

Finally, I had envisioned a closed class with a definite start and end date (mostly to be able to synthesize the lessons). Staff at the work furlough program suggested instead that the class be open-ended and that each session should last one hour and that attendance should be voluntary. Staff felt that participation would be sporadic at best and that residents would eventually become uninterested or inattentive during long classes. Soon after the classes began it became clear that the students were highly motivated. As the weeks progressed, the number of women who attended the class continued to grow, and by the end, thirty-four out of fifty residents (68%) attended between one and three classes. Of the thirty-four, eighteen students (53%) attended regularly and for more hours than required for their individual programs.[6] What was the appeal?

Based on student feedback from short (voluntary) class evaluations and a final survey, several factors contributed to the success of the class.[7] For example, one question in the survey asked, "What barriers prevent imprisoned people from taking courses like this?" The majority of respondents noted that the content was new and therefore interesting, and that they "want to learn more." Several commented that prison bureaucracies did not allow "this kind of knowledge," because it was "too threatening for the system if people understand what's happening." One woman appropriately stated, "It's just like they just only want to teach us cognitive skills stuff so we keep only looking at ourselves and not the big picture. When you see the big picture, it's just like you want to do better, cuz you know everything is not just your fault."

Apparently, course content opened space for people to connect or disconnect their lives from larger systemic issues, and exposure to new knowledge stimulated learning. The second factor (based on student comments throughout the course) was that students appreciated combining theory with practice through participatory lessons. For example, students at first expressed that they viewed politics as an entity for corruption and a space inaccessible to them. As the classes progressed and certainly by the end of the pilot, students not only saw themselves as political actors and their everyday lives as political, but also had a desire to become change agents through various political processes. Half of the classes were held in the community and included attending plays, cultural and historical walking tours, archival/genealogical research, and indigenous story-telling and music events, among other activities. In-class lessons combined lectures with hands-on learning assignments, including an educational overview of legislative processes, researching and writing letters to the editor and opinion editorials, Hawaiian history and politics, felony disenfranchisement and non-partisan voter rights, and completing college applica-

---

6    Students were between 29 and 52 years old, with a median age of 40. Of the 34 students, 18 reported being Hawaiian or part-Hawaiian. Twenty-three out of thirty-four students were mothers of at least one child.

7    Seventeen out of eighteen students in regular attendance completed surveys. The eighteenth student was returned to prison before the conclusion of the class.

tions and writing personal statements for scholarships. Students commented that they were "no longer afraid of politics" and many felt that attending community classes "with other women made it easier to go back into the community." Students repeatedly requested that the classes be longer in length and time. Several expressed frustration that they were never told that so many community resources were available to them and their children, often asking "How come nobody told us this information?"

There were many milestones throughout the pilot. For example, five students applied to college. Three of the women who wrote their personal statements in the college overview class secured financial aid and private scholarships. Fourteen women registered to vote for the 2008 election. One student learned that she had a natural ability to conduct qualitative research during the genealogy class at the state archives and public library and is now working at a research institution. During the class on writing letters to the editor, one group wrote a publishable article while another conducted further in-depth research on federal wiretapping in order to construct their arguments regarding the policy. Prior to a historical walking tour in Waikīkī, some students expressed trepidation about going into the area because of pre-imprisonment experiences. Afterwards, they stated that they were "less afraid" because they could draw from a different view of the place as one that was culturally sacred. This leads to the third component of success. There was a level of trust that obviously developed throughout the pilot. Three qualities in particular that shaped our learning community were respect, motivation, and liberation. Of course, there were many other elements that made this experience successful, but I emphasize these qualities, because they reflect general comments expressed by the students and my own personal observations.

We live under a regime of deliberate silence regarding the standardized containment and punishment of entire groups of people. Society continues to create policies and practices that define certain groups as criminal and devise solutions for saving members of these groups from themselves. These policies and practices utterly fail to produce public safety. And they both create and ignore the institutionalized terror against marginalized communities. The unique political history and status of Hawaiians lends rare insight into the way in which state violence is rooted in colonialism. Anti-hegemonic discourses and political activism are critical if we are to reverse these trends. Without exception, this project requires new approaches to reentry in Hawai'i and abroad. Going forward, our goals must be to increase political literacy and create ways of hearing, understanding and responding to the voices and experiences of those most intimately familiar with the prison industrial complex.

RAEDEEN KEAHIOLALO-KARASUDA *is a doctoral candidate in Political Science at the University of Hawai'i-Mānoa. Her nearly-completed dissertation research links the colonial history of Hawaiians to the ever-expanding prison industrial complex. She has been an Open Society Institute Soros Justice Fellow since 2007. This essay was made possible with the generous support of the Open Society Institute's Soros Justice Fellowship.*

## REFERENCES

Adrian, Manuella. 2002. "A Critical Perspective on Cross-Cultural Contexts for Addiction and Multiculturalism: Their Meanings and Implications in the Substance Abuse Field." *Substance Abuse & Misuse* 37, no. 8–10 (2002): 853–900.

Allen, Helena G. *The Betrayal of Liliuokalani: Last Queen of Hawaii 1838–1917.* Honolulu: Mutual Publishing, 1982.

———. *Kalakaua: Renaissance King.* Honolulu: Mutual Publishing, 1994.

Brown, Marilyn. "Aina Under the Influence: The Criminalization of Alcohol in 19th-Century Hawai'i." *Theoretical Criminology* 7, no.1'(2003): 89–110.

Christian, Johnna R. *Exploring the Effects of Incarceration on Communities.* Dissertation. State University of New York, Albany, 2004.

Cook, Bud Pomaika'i, Kelley Withy, and Lucia Tarallo-Jensen. "Cultural Trauma, Hawaiian Spirituality, and Contemporary Health Status." *California Journal of Health Promotion 2003* 1 (Special Issue: Hawai'i): 10–24.

Cunningham, Dennis. *Cross Continental Cross Cultural Corporation.* Oklahoma Department of Corrections, n.d.

Davis, Angela Y. *Are Prisons Obscolete?* New York: Seven Stories Press, 2003.

Dayton, Kevin. "Arizona Prison in Turmoil." *The Honolulu Advertiser,* July 1, 2001.

———. "A Decade of Hawai'i's Prison Policy: Potential Costs More than Money." *The Honolulu Advertiser,* October 2, 2005.

———. "Inmate's Death in Ky. to Be Probed." *The Honolulu Advertiser,* June 13, 2006.

———. "Hawai'i prison inmates moved to Arizona." *The Honolulu Advertiser*, September 29, 2006.

———. "Another Inmate Injured in Lockdown Breach." *The Honolulu Advertiser*, July 13, 2007.

Foucault, Michel. *Discipline and Punish: The Birth of the Prison*. New York: Vintage Books, 1977.

Frank, Clayton. Written Comments on Senate Bill 2342 SD2 Relating to the Auditor, edited by D. o. P. Safety: Hawai'i State Legislature. March 31, 2008.

Gilmore, Ruth Wilson. "Race and Globalization." In *Geographies of Global Change: Remapping the World*, edited by R.J. Johnston, Peter J. Taylor, and Michael J. Watts. Oxford: Blackwell, 2002.

Hallett, Michael. "Commerce with Criminals: The New Colonialism in Criminal Justice." *Review of Policy Research* 21, no. 1 (2004): 49–62.

Hishinuma, Earl S., et al. 2005. "Prevalence and Correlates of Misconduct Among Ethnically Diverse Adolescents of Native Hawaiian/Part-Hawaiian and Non-Hawaiian Ancestry." *International Journal of Social Psychiatry* 51, no. 3 (2005): 242–258.

Irwin, Bernice Piilani. *I Knew Queen Lili'uokalani*. Honolulu: First People's Production, 1960.

Kame'eleihiwa, Lilikalä. *Native Land and Foreign Desires: Pehea Lä E Pono Ai?* Honolulu: Bishop Museum Press, 1992.

Kana'iaupuni, Shawn, Nolan Malone, and Koren Ishibashi. 2005. *Ka Huaka'i: Native Hawaiian Educational Assessment*. Honolulu: Kamehameha Schools, 2005.

Karasuda, RaeDeen, and Katherine Irwin. 2005, September 5. "Dog's 'Tough Love' on Crime Isn't Helping." *The Honolulu Advertiser*, September 5, 2005.

Kauanui, J. Kehaulani. "The Politics of Blood and Sovereignty in *Rice v. Cayetano*." *Association for Political and Legal Anthropology* 25, no. 1 (2002): 110–128.

Kaulukukui, Guy H. "Hawaiian Vote Carried Hanneman. *The Honolulu Advertiser*, Novemeber 28, 2004.

Keahiolalo-Karasuda, RaeDeen M. "Hawaiians (Ethnic) and Incarceration." In *Battleground: Criminal Justice*, edited by G. Barak. Westport: Greenwood Press, 2007.

*Lili'uokalani v. The United States*. 1910.

Lili'uokalani. *Hawai'i's Story by Hawai'i's Queen*. Honolulu: Mutual Publishing, 1990.

Marez, Curtis. *Drug Wars: The Political Economy of Narcotics*. Minneapolis: University of Minnesota Press, 2004.

Mauer, Marc, and U.S. Sentencing Project. *Race to Incarcerate*. New York: New Press, 1999.

Merry, Sally Engle. *Colonizing Hawai'i: The Cultural Power of Law* (Princeton Studies in Culture/ Power/History). Princeton, NJ: Princeton University Press, 2000.

———. "Crime and Criminality: Historical Differences in Hawai'i." *The Contemporary Pacific* 14 (2002): 412–424.

*Olim v. Wakinekona,* 461 U.S. 238; 103 S. Ct. 1741; 75 L. Ed. 2d 813. 1983.

Osorio, Jon Kay Kamakawiwo'ole. *Dismembering Lāhui: A History of the Hawaiian Nation to 1887.* Honolulu: University of Hawai'i Press, 2002.

Silva, Noenoe K. *Aloha Betrayed: Native Hawaiian Resistance to American Colonialism.* Durham & London: Duke University Press, 2004.

Star-Bulletin Staff. Untitled. *Star-Bulletin*, May 5, 1975.

State of Hawai'i Department of Public Safety (DPS). *Annual Report.* Honolulu: Department of Public Safety, 2003.

Talvi, Silija J.A. "No Room in Prison? Ship 'Em Off: Prisoners Have Become Unwitting Pawns in a Lowest-Bidder-Gets-the-Convict Shuffle Game." *In These Times*, May 10, 2006.

Towse, Ed. *The Rebellion of 1895: A Complete History of the Insurrection against the Republic of Hawaii.* Honolulu: The Hawaiian Star, 1895.

Trask, Haunani-Kay. "Tourist, Stay Home." *Progressive* 57, no. 7 (1993).

———. *From a Native Daughter: Colonialism and Sovereignty in Hawai'i*, Rev. ed. Honolulu: University of Hawai'i Press, 1999.

———. 2000. "Native Social Capital: The Case of Hawaiian Sovereignty and Ka Lahui Hawai'i." *Policy Sciences* 33 (2000): 375–385.

Travis, Jeremy, and Michelle Waul. *Prisoners Once Removed: The Impact of Incarceration and Reentry on Children, Families, and Communities.* Washington: The Urban Institute Press, 2003.

Vorsino, Mary. "Foster Program Helps Native Hawaiian Kids." *Star-Bulletin*, July 11, 2005.

*Wakinekona v. Olim,* 459 F. Supp. 473; 1978 U.S. Dist. LEXIS 17304. 1978. United States District Court for the District of Hawaii.

*Wakinekona v. Olim,* 664 F.2d 708; 1981 U.S. App. LEXIS 12948. 1981. United States Court of Appeals, Ninth Circuit.

# PRISON ABOLITION IN PRACTICE: THE LEAD PROJECT, THE POLITICS OF HEALING AND "A NEW WAY OF LIFE"

*Setsu Shigematsu, Gwen D'Arcangelis, and Melissa Burch*

In 1982, in a residential neighborhood in Los Angeles, a speeding police car hit a five year old boy and killed him. Susan Burton, the mother of this five year old, experienced the agony of losing her son because of this preventable "police incident". Without a supportive family or community around her, and a police force that failed to offer even an apology for killing her son, this loss added to already difficult factors in Susan's life to produce a devastating effect. Turning to means deemed "illegal" by the State to lessen her pain and grief resulted in Susan's imprisonment on drug related charges. For the next decade, Susan was in and out of prison, her life becoming one of millions caught in the vicious cycle of the penal system. Fifteen years later, she was finally admitted to an effective rehabilitation program and was on the road to her recovery.

*How can women whose lives have been most adversely impacted by the penal system, transform themselves and be transformed through a politics of prison abolition?*

In 1999, with her own recovery underway, Susan went on to found "A New Way of Life," a group of transition homes for women coming home from prison in the Watts District of Los Angeles. Susan's life reveals how an abolitionist perspective works to transform the lives of women impacted by the prison system. In our view, abolition is not only a political ideal, but also a practice that creates new kinds of communities. This article elaborates how prison abolition works to transform and heal lives. We focus on the transformation of Susan Burton and the Leadership, Education, Action and Dialogue (LEAD) Project—a political education program that fosters critical analysis of the prison industrial complex. The LEAD Project grew out of a collaboration of "A New Way of Life" and the Los Angeles chapter of "Critical Resistance" an abolitionist organization that Susan began working with in 2003.

## FROM CAPTIVE TO FIGHTER: ONE WOMAN'S STORY

It was soon after Susan became sober and began to work in her community to aid elderly African Americans who were suffering from health problems that she learned about the growing numbers of incarcerated women and how they too faced the daunting systemic conditions that she herself had confronted. She decided to do something about it. In 1999, Susan was able to obtain a home in Watts that she opened to women coming home from prison and women on probation and parole. This was the beginning of what would become "A New Way of Life," a group of nonprofit sober living and transition homes.

On any given day in Los Angeles County, there are 3,000 women on parole. About half of them have the disease of drug addiction and live in South Central Los Angeles. Close to 70% will go back to prison, either convicted of a new crime or failing to meet the conditions of parole within a year of their release. Often unable or unwilling to attain assistance from agencies perceived as insensitive and judgmental and which have highly structured programs that restrict individual choice, the women struggle to stay out of prison, to find legal income, and to remain sober in isolation.

In contrast, Susan's homes offer a clean, safe, supportive environment for women coming home from jail or prison. One resident describes the environment at A New Way of Life (NWOL):

> She [Susan] helped me get a job, and now I have a steady job ... She made me feel welcome, I can't explain it, she just taught me so much and made me feel comfortable; it's really hard for me to open up to people, but she really made me feel like she cared about me and wanted me to get clean, instead of just trying to make money off of me.

While supporting women struggle to put their lives back together, Susan repeatedly witnessed them losing their children to the foster care system because they couldn't meet the state's requirements for reunification. Susan experienced their pain and her loss over again:

It was devastating to watch women lose their children when they were doing everything they possibly could ... But to see that happen and understand what it felt like to lose a child, I felt it over and over again, and that was enough to give me the fire, the determination, the commitment to address it and it was against all odds ... I was so angry at the system that I was going to walk through hell and high water in order to make a difference.

Susan has been able to work out of the pain, anger and grief to create a remarkable home for women to be reunited with their children after suffering from the multifaceted disruption and break-up of the family imposed through the prison and police system. In addition to providing the necessities of housing, food, clothing, transportation and health care, A New Way of Life (NWOL) began programs to help women access case management services, job training, skill-building, and community advocacy opportunities. Alongside the development of A New Way of Life (NWOL), Susan became increasingly involved in working toward systemic changes to address the injustices she was witnessing on a daily basis, and soon became a leading advocate in California for the rights of former prisoners.

In 2003, Susan participated in the Critical Resistance South conference in New Orleans, Louisiana. Her encounter with Critical Resistance would prove to be a pivotal experience. Founded in 1998, Critical Resistance (CR) is a member-led organization that seeks to abolish the prison industrial complex (PIC)—in other words, to end the use of prisons and policing as ineffective and dehumanizing responses to social and economic problems. Through grassroots campaigns and projects, CR works to challenge the notion that caging and controlling people makes us safer, and to build a national movement)—guided by those most impacted by the system—to promote and realize genuine forms of safety and security.

Recalling when she first met CR members, and came to understand their abolitionist stance she says,

I didn't have a concept as wonderful as that ... I had never heard anyone challenge prisons in the way that CR challenges the existence of prisons period. To understand and to know that a prison is not a solution, what a prison does to people is torture—this should be prohibited. It should not be able to function ... And then to begin to imagine a world without prisons ... there's so many other ways to treat people.

Susan readily states that when she first got involved in community activism she did not have a complete analysis of the interconnections between the prison industrial complex and the other systemic forms of oppression. Her exposure to CR's analysis of the prison industrial complex, and her own development of an abolitionist perspective set the stage for the formation of the LEAD Project.

## THE VISION AND PRACTICE OF LEAD

In 2004, Susan met Critical Resistance (CR) organizer Melissa Burch through mutual anti-PIC activism in Los Angeles. As they began to share their political visions, Melissa conceived of the idea to start a political education program at a New Way of Life. Susan wholeheartedly collaborated. Melissa along with a few other CR members began to design workshops to critically analyze the PIC with A New Way of Life residents.

The women who live at A New Way of Life (NWOL) and participate in the LEAD Project have all had personal experiences with the effects of the criminal justice system on their lives and on the lives of their loved ones. Most of the women at NWOL are low-income African-American women, a population increasingly affected by the PIC. Although the number of imprisoned men is much higher, African American women represent the fastest growing population of prisoners in the US today. Over the past 18 years, we have witnessed an astounding 800% increase in rates of imprisonment for women of color. Driven largely by the so-called "war on drugs," the majority of these women remain behind bars on small-scale drug charges, the result of a system less interested in treating addiction than in punishing those who do not have the social, economic, and political clout to keep themselves out of prison. Through educating about the history and politics of the prison industrial complex, LEAD exposes how the system operates—not to prosecute all forms of "crime'—but to target and entrap only certain groups of people. One woman tells her story:

> I was at the can place, at the recycling, and this girl was going to do the recycling for me, because I couldn't go in, because me and the recycling lady didn't get along, so she took the cans and bottles in there for me, she took my cans and bottles in there, she came outside and gave me 2 dollars and 5 cents. A police car drives by and sees her handing me the money, they made a U-turn and came back, and then a bunch more police cars came and jacked me up, and said I have 'possession of sales'. I couldn't argue the case because they said they seen her hand me the money. It was 2 dollars and 5cents for my cans and bottles. I'm right in front of the can place! The people at the can place even tried to tell them [that I was recycling cans], but they [the police] said, "No, she was buying dope!" So I went to jail with 2 dollars and 5 cents on my books for possession of sales.

Through bi-weekly participatory workshops, the LEAD project creates a space in which women who have recently been released from prison can temporarily step outside conventional recovery programs' emphasis on the personal and look critically at the larger social and political systems that perpetuate the prison in-dustrial complex. Drawing on the women's own experiences with the system, the LEAD Project further exposes how the penal system works to label certain groups of people as "convicts" or "felons," a status that simultaneously impacts one's sense of self-worth and cuts off a person's opportunities to lead a healthy economically self-sustaining life.

The LEAD project works toward a women-of-color centered critique of the prison industrial complex, emphasizing how it is an extension of the interlocking racist, heterosexist, and classist forms of systemic oppression. The workshops offer a critique of various interconnected aspects of the prison industrial complex (PIC), such as the "war on drugs" and the arbitrary construction of "crime." In each work-shop, LEAD organizers facilitate a number of activities that include role-playing, films, guided discussion, small group work, guest speakers, journal writing and life history exercises, to help participants make the connections between the PIC and the systemic conditions of their own imprisonment, probation/parole status. Other projects of LEAD that foster political education and leadership development include the maintenance of a political education media library and a grassroots organizing internship focusing on collective engagement in community actions.

In this way, LEAD offers an organic extension of Susan's own experience and politicization, as well as an extension of CR's abolitionist vision in practice. By em-phasizing learning about, envisioning and practicing alternative forms of justice and safety, LEAD instantiates abolition in the present by resisting a narrow reliance on the state that dictates punitive forms of justice. Instead, LEAD seeks to imple-ment restorative forms of community-based justice and rehabilitation. By collec-tively imagining what changes would be necessary to create truly safe and secure communities, the LEAD project offers a vision of justice that is based on the well-being of entire communities.

## HEALING, TRANSFORMATION, AND ABOLITION

It takes quite a bit of energy and belief in yourself and willingness to open your mind to make that transition from *captive to someone who is going to fight* … It takes a bit of commitment and force within yourself to come out and do that, after living in that place of less than, and not-good-enough.

As exemplified in Susan's story, a new understanding of the system is integral to the process of reevaluating the conditions of one's incarceration and vital to the process of healing and the determination to fight an oppressive system. The LEAD project offers women this space to critically dialogue about their experiences. Many of the women at A New Way of Life (NWOL) describe the particularities of a criminal justice system that serves to help keep them in an incarceration cycle. Instead of offering treatment, the system penalizes these women who lack the resources to escape such entrapment; says one woman, "Don't just drag 25 people where the only crime they had was getting high, and then you give them 4 years in prison, and then you release them out into society with nothing ... you're just making it a revolving door. You let them out with nothing." Susan emphasizes that healing from the denigration, abuse and dehumanization enacted from the system requires new forms of knowledge and the *time and space* for each person to recover. The LEAD project plays a key role in pushing the women through the very difficult, but essential transition that shifts the blame from "it's me" to "it's the system." It is this understanding that Susan believes is necessary to move oneself away from the self-destructive tendencies that lead to addictions and "self-abuse". This opportunity and ability to reevaluate oneself from this political perspective can be key to rebuilding self-worth, and the successful transition to leading a healthy life.

One woman explains the role of a NWOL and her education through participating in the LEAD workshops as key to her empowerment and transition to healthier living: "I didn't realize things like CR [Critical Resistance] actually existed. I didn't know that there were people out there trying to stop it or reform it ... people who have never been incarcerated, never been in trouble, and they're out there fighting against something that's wrong. So CR, all of that showed me something different, that I do have a say and that my voice can make a difference in a lot of things."

## BUILDING A MOVEMENT

For Susan, and for many women at A New Way of Life (NWOL), a new understanding of the system has been integral to the process of reevaluating the conditions of their own incarceration and vital to the process of healing. Over the course of seven years, since its opening, Susan's program has touched the lives of over 250 women. Through their experience at a NWOL and the political education provided by the LEAD Project, many women have not only begun to feel more empowered to stand up and fight but are now also able to view the problems of the PIC and envision alternatives. One resident says: "I think that the way that it is right now ... just needs to be completely abolished. I am not saying that we do not need some kind of system in place but the one that we have we do not need." Another resident speaks to her vision of safe communities:

> They should build more of these [NWOL] than prisons. Because when I got here it was like a new world to me. I was glad and ... It wasn't like being locked in; there were restrictions, but still, I wasn't locked in. I could go outside and smoke a cigarette. I could do this, I could do that. I was gonna go back to school. She [Susan] showed me a school, got me an ID and Social Security card, things I didn't have she showed me how to get them. It was like starting all over again in a new world. If they had more places like A New Way of Life, they would have better communities, I believe.

Many of the women at a NWOL have even taken the political education one step further, and like Susan, are transforming themselves into leaders in the movement against the PIC. Several are active in the local chapter of "All of us or None," a former prisoner led initiative to end discrimination against former prisoners in jobs, education, and access to services. Some have become involved in efforts to stop prison expansion in California, while others have become active in different arenas of the struggle for social justice. While it takes time, even years, for a person to heal and recover, Susan's life story attests to how a successful transition from the denigrating effects of prison-life back to leading a healthy life often requires a form of self-reevaluation that is at once political, emotional and spiritual. A politics of abolition can be practiced as part of this process of personal healing. Susan and many of the other women at a NWOL have come to embody this vision of healing and transformation that offers a radically new perspective on themselves, their place in the world, and the possibility of a future without prisons.

SETSU SHIGEMATSU *and* GWEN D'ARCANGELIS *are co-organizers with* MELISSA BURCH, *who established the LEAD Project.*

*This article is reprinted from* Interrupted Life: Experiences of Incarcerated Mothers in the United States. *Forthcoming from University of California Press in spring 2008, the book addresses issues related to experiences and policies regarding women's incarceration. It includes essays, poetry, and other contributions. The book will be published in the United States and will be sold in the United States and other countries. It may be excerpted in newspapers and magazines, and it may later be published in other editions, including book club editions and foreign language translations, and in electronic and other media.*

# FREEDOM SEEDS: GROWING ABOLITION IN DURHAM, NORTH CAROLINA

*Alexis Pauline Gumbs*

What if abolition isn't a shattering thing, not a crashing thing, not a wrecking ball event? What if abolition is something that sprouts out of the wet places in our eyes, the broken places in our skin, the waiting places in our palms, the tremble holding in my mouth when I turn to you? What if abolition is something that grows? What if abolishing the prison industrial complex is the fruit of our diligent gardening, building and deepening of a movement to respond to the violence of the state and the violence in our communities with sustainable, transformative love?

In Durham, North Carolina there is a garden in a neighborhood torn apart by rape, and the support of rape, and the silencing of survivors. There is a garden in a neighborhood that is likewise torn apart by policing and imprisonment and the de-humanization of people who experience the threat and threads of being locked up, and watched every day. In this particular soil, sharp, red, sticky with the afterlife of slavery and a system of white supremacy enforced by sexual and physical violence against many people for many generations, something else is growing. Alternate routes are embracing each other underground; bursts of truth are flowering to the surface.

In the wake of a recently highly publicized rape trial, where women of color, sex workers and survivors of sexual violence were criminalized for speaking their truths, Durham North Carolina is growing. In April 2006 when a student at North Carolina Central University who was also a mother, an exotic dancer, and a Black woman reported an incident of sexual violence that occurred at a Duke Lacrosse Team party in a house owned by the University, a community full of survivors of sexual violence, women of color, mothers, sex workers and allies were retraumatized by the hateful responses of the University, the local and national media and the state, which unsurprisingly had no accountability to the woman who reported the crime.

In this devastating and extremely violent period community organizers and artists in Durham, learned, through fire, the central role of sexual violence in the linked oppressions that we experience and the urgent need for healing and justice in our communities. A coalition called UBUNTU, named for the African concept "I am because we are" was born at this time, and a year later in collaboration with 8 other groups we created a healing, poetic vigil, march and celebration of survival called the National Day of Truthtelling that transformed and revealed the landscape of our city.

Caitlin Breedlove, founding member of UBUNTU and co-director of Southerners on New Ground (two of the organizations that created the Day of Truthtelling), explains the Day of Truthtelling, as a national event organized by a broad coalition of 9 groups based in and around Durham, North Carolina; the Day of Truthtelling was more than a visible marker of resistance, and more than an intentional statement against sexual violence.

The result of that event is a community that reaches to live up to the world made possible through the creative, analytical and physical expressions made on that day. The organizing that went into the Day of Truthtelling, and the continued grassroots responses to violence that follow it, make it possible to imagine a city that has been operating on a plantation model of racism, terror, and the production of fear-enforced compliance in a new way. Breedlove explains that the Day of Truthtelling

is also a geography of a town re-imagined by survivors, and a resiliency of a group of people who stood up to a lot of hate mail and hate expression to speak our truth. No one can take what we learned away from us.

In the dwelling place of all our tears, our wounds, our rage, hope and intention, there is a garden growing literally and figuratively. It remains to be seen if this garden can feed us. It remains to be seen if this garden will replace our consumption of social products (like fear) that eat our bodies from the inside out. It remains to be seen what we will become, but for sure, growth is present. In this article, we present strategies for responding to violence without re-enforcing the prison industrial complex. Our struggle is a garden and our experience so far, while specific to this very soil, may be useful as a model for those elsewhere who struggle to create a world free from sexual, and state violence. The order of these gardening actions is not completely arbitrary, but we want you to know that what we are describing is not a straight line forward from breaking the ground to sharing the harvest. The work of growing works in cycles of effort sustained by the belief that life is both unpredictable and possible in every moment.

## 1. BREAK GROUND: UNEARTHING POSSIBILITY

Reflect on the place you stand. Maybe the ground you stand on is thick with screams, hard with the caked silences of those who resigned themselves to pain. Maybe the ground you stand on has been forced for centuries to bear a product that cannot feed anyone, transitioning morbidly from tobacco to silence. Maybe the land here has been stripped for the production of individualism. What grows here chokes everyone, whether it is the bright leaves of tobacco or the shiny narrative of sports heroes, winners and losers, university students primed to market themselves as people who will not talk about their own pain, or the pain of others.

Sylvia Wynter explains that what differentiates the plantations from other forms of growing is that the growth of the plantation depends on the demands of a removed market, not the needs of the people who eat, live, and breathe on the same land. And no one can eat tobacco anyway. This is why near the fields of every plantation there are also gardens, plots of land, tended in the off time, threatened by the secondary status of human life. There is always something else growing here, even if it only barely keeps us from starving.

Reflect on the place you stand and what makes it stable, what makes it whole. Here in Durham it is blood and silence. It is the theft of whole lifetimes into caged survival and exploited labor. It is the mantra that the only way to win is by dominating someone else—with your brain, or your body, or your basketball record. It is the silence of the losses that we swallow when our loved ones are stolen and our bodies are transformed into dirt for each other to walk upon.

This ground has been land for sacrifice of bodies to capital. The discourse following the Duke Lacrosse case sought to maintain and resecure that purpose. As Caitlin Breedlove explains, the seeds of violence are everywhere in Durham: "It is located everywhere, unfortunately. We hold it in our bodies, families, communities, streets, houses, and trees."

Reflect on the place you stand. Now bend and shovel through the surface, turning land over until the danger is revealed. Truth is, violence is not the only thing growing here; the one crop economy is a lie. Truth is, there is another kind of richness in this soil when you turn it over. Lynne Walter, member of UBUNTU and organizer of the Day of Truthtelling points out:

We need to flip that kind of thinking around and take the fact that the multiple levels of violence are all interconnected and work it to our advantage. Understanding that affecting positive social change at the institutional level can impact people's thoughts and beliefs, and that how working with individuals around how they can end violence will impact other levels is much more of a positive frame and will help us stay strong.

This dirt is as strong as we are, as full of alternative histories and forgotten resistance as our skin cells. The place that you stand is ready with queer potentials that contradict the market that has been draining it all this time. In our case, the landscape depicted through the cruel and ongoing relationship between an elitist university and a working class employed by that elitist community is also a place where people have been growing their plots. Where Nia Wilson works at the overpriced Whole Foods to make time so she can grow the organization SpiritHouse, which she directs. Where elementary art teacher Malcolm Goff makes murals about the deadly legacy of tobacco in the late night and early morning hours. Where Afiya Carter makes the brave choice to abandon her job as an executive for the biotechnology industry in our region in order to create community cultural events that feed the people nutritionally and spiritually. Where Mama Vimala creates an alternative economy based on delicious Indian dinners prepared at her home. Where there is still a chapter of Marcus Garvey's U.N.I.A. Where graduate students steal billions of photocopies to publish workbooks and pamphlets. Where an interracial group of 6 lesbians founded an organization committed to addressing welfare reform and immigration policy as crucial issues in the fight for queer liberation. Where there is more than one West African dance instructor per square mile. Where a young Palestinian woman has been running the main Latino community center, for years with loving success. Where, quiet as it's kept, the people who run the community organizations, the state agencies, and the local publications are survivors and co-survivors of gendered violence; we are discovering the bankruptcies of our silence. Durham is a queer place if you look a little bit deeper. Bet the place you live is too. Dig deep.

*In order to respond to violence without reinforcing the prison industrial complex it is crucial to turn over the soil of our communities to see what is buried and growing there. What has been silenced because of its danger? What do mainstream representations of our city try to forget? These are our primary resources.*

Reflect on the place that you stand and turn it over with the names of the ancestors who fought here, turn it over to the rhythm of the silences that allowed people to survive, turn it over the in memory of queer love and struggle that was buried here. This is the queer thing. Everything that has been buried still lives. Everything that is suppressed is waiting in the soil, ready for our need. Dig deep and turn it over, turn it over, turn it over, turn it over.

## 2. FEED THE SOIL: SUSTAINING COMMUNITY

Centuries of violence drain a place. Fueling our alternative and urgent service oriented projects while constantly repressing the impact of gendered violence on our lives is draining. Trauma invades our dreams at night, our relationships, our health and our imaginations. We are parched, mal-nourished, often running on empty. UBUNTU means "I am because we are," which means we are tired because our communities, especially our Black, Latino, queer, and working class communities here in Durham are exhausted, overworked, under-rewarded, and kept awake at night because of the constant threat of imprisonment. Our tendency to burn out as organizers is related to the impoverishment of our communities on every level.

In order to revitalize the suppressed roots of transformation in our communities, we have to feed each other in every way possible. In a recent interview for *Revolution at Home*, a zine by Leah Lakshmi Piepzna Samarasinha about partner violence in activist communities, UBUNTU explained the importance of a community building presence, describing the way UBUNTU participates in community activities that don't seem directly related to sexual violence prevention and response:

> UBUNTU in partnership with SpiritHouse and Southerners on New Ground has started doing community dinners at W.D. Hill (a local community center at which one of our members is an employee) which lets people know that this work exists as a tangible resource. UBUNTU has been strongly present at important community celebrations from Kwanzaa to "community day" to the MLK celebration which builds the message that since there are people in this community who will gather when we need, face-painting, food, art, or people power to get something done, and since these folks (us!) are specifically about (and always talking about) responding to violence, that means there is a community of support available to help me respond to violence.

The process of feeding the general community and sustaining a community of organizers is directly linked because everyone is a potential organizer for their own liberation. UBUNTU has built relationships that also allow us to create resources to feed the spirits of those of us facing our biggest fears while organizing against gendered violence and the violence of the state as people who have been traumatized by multiple forms of violence ourselves. Therefore:

> UBUNTU also functions as a site of sustainability in another sense. The fact that we have built informal mechanisms to offer childcare, trade massages, do aromatherapy work, share personal fitness training, cook for each other, grow food together, help with homework, borrow cars, offer a space to crash means that as each of us takes seriously the work of responding to violence in our scattered communities as teachers, organizers, immigrants rights activists, we also have a support network to help us, feed us, hug us, massage us, create a healing oil for us, write a poem about our name, make a cup of tea when we need it. And we often do. We need it almost everyday.

*If we can feed and sustain each other, we have less need to call on or depend on the state or the status quo. The knowledge that we have communities of support can awaken our bravery and ignite our imaginations for a transformed world.*

## 3. KISS THE ROUTES: COALITIONAL STRATEGIES

Under the ground there is a complicated set of connections, so planting our work in a specific community context means acknowledging those connections. Durham is a relatively small community; so alongside the transient population of students, there are long-standing relationships generations deep between elders and babies. Grandmothers, mothers, and daughters organize together. Sisters work on executive boards together. Godparents and aunties are the hinges of intergenerational community initiatives. We are all eating out of the same plate; and the size and economy of our city makes this impossible to ignore.

The depressed economic situation that Durham shares with other post-industrial southern cities and the University-centered economy of the city (in tandem with the prison industrial complex-dependent economy of the state) creates a competitive environment where official non-profit organizations fight for a very limited set of resources. At the same time, the existence of a close-knit activist community also means that when people harm each other, through oppressive organizational practices, fighting over scraps, or interpersonal lack of accountability the fallout is intense.

While our activist community here is sustained by long and emerging relationships, it is also fractured by old and new divisions between individuals and initiatives. In order to create responses to violence that do not operate through the channels of the prison industrial complex, it is crucial that we acknowledge and affirm the relationships that transcend and underpin the institutional alliances in our activist communities. These relationships are our pathways to freedom, our revolutionary routes.

Here in Durham it has been crucial that our response to violence has operated in coalition; not only because specific organizations have experience addressing the different manifestations of violence that support rape culture, but also to make space for the leadership of people directly impacted by these different issues, and also because our interconnectedness allows us to access resources in ways that are not limited to the chain of command and the ultimate prison pipeline that the state has set up to respond to violence.

For example, since UBUNTU is a coalition, it consists of many individuals and some organizational entities. Organizations such as SpiritHouse, Southerners on New Ground, and Men Against Rape Culture bring specific analytic tools and histories of fighting racist, homophobic and gendered violence in a way that is explicitly critical of the state. Some of the organizations that UBUNTU works with closely, such as North Carolina Coalition Against Sexual Assault and Orange County Rape Crisis Center are direct service providers that respond to individual crises, but who are largely dependent on the limits of the State. The coalitional space of UBUNTU, and the relationships between the individual workers at these agencies, allow us access to much of the legal and organizational information that help us to navigate situations of violence, even when those experiencing it cannot depend directly to the service providers because of the way that the racism, classism and nativism of government leak through state-dependent anti-violence agencies. Also, this coalitional relationship (with organizations that are part of UBUNTU and also with organizations that are not officially part of UBUNTU but have worked with us in coalition on projects (including the National Day of Truthtelling) means that the political visioning and creative work that we do influences the work of those organizations. And people who end up connected with those service providers also have access to the work of UBUNTU, as a survivor led space of continued healing through the process of building community.

One UBUNTU member says, "We are not concretely 'providing services,' but from our experiences so far, I feel that we are linked to a set of organizational histories, networks and resources that make me confident when someone calls in a state of emergency that I have a rich set of resources to offer them, from legal help, to relocation assistance, to a breathing circle, to a poem, to medical attention, to a meal.

Since we are not linked to the state we have the potential to provide people with a more robust set of options that can respond to their needs and desires, and I think that is important ... especially for womyn and trans folks of color and immigrants who have such good reasons to avoid the retraumatizing impact of the state."

*Kissing the routes means prioritizing strategy and nurturing relationships that allow us the maximum number of options when we are addressing a specific instance of violence. And ultimately the route to our shared freedom and healing is through organizing.*

As Caitlin Breedlove emphasizes:

We have created a space where people who do not have access and are not comfortable with service providers to address their survivor issues, could get peer support. This is invaluable for some of us—for example, sex workers and former sex workers—who so often feel that service provision is not a place where we can be honest, open, heard, and understood. We must re-imagine what 'service' is, when it is so unempowering for so many. The role of any service provision, or advocacy, as we create a new society should be to supporting healing through organizing—as this encourages all oppressed people to take power back.

### 3. HANDS INTO THE EARTH: COMPLICITY AND ACCOUNTABILITY

It's unavoidable. Growth means getting our hands dirty, or understanding how dirty they already are. *In order to connect with our routes, to dig deep, to plant and nurture growing life we have to be real about the complexity of our own actions. This means being specific about our relationships to the state, this means acknowledging that we are all capable of harming each other even when we don't mean to. This means the difficult remembering that if most perpetrators of gendered violence have survived violence themselves, those of us who identify as survivors have often been perpetrators in a number of ways.* This means acknowledging that the free or cheap materials we have access to come at the expense of someone's exploited labor. This means remembering the impact our computers have on the environment and on the fingers of the people piecing them together even as we organize on facebook.

Acknowledging that "I am Because We Are" or that all of our actions impact each other is fundamental to creating accountability. When we take a stance that says that we will go for the root cause and not criminalize each other for harmful actions that are already linked to wider structures of harm and processes of growth and learning, we can free each other to take responsibility for harmful actions that occur in our communities instead of trying to fabricate an impossible innocence. I am because we are. This means we are all necessary to each other and we are all involved in each other's actions for worse and also for better.

Our hands are dirty but they are warm because of their connection to the earth our shared context. We are in the messy everyday of each other, we cannot remain clean, but we can hold each other accountable to learn from our mistakes, to hold ourselves to ever more intentional levels of engagement. We can be partners in radical healing, which means addressing the root causes of the harms we endure at each other's hands.

## 4. WATER AND SUNLIGHT: HEALING AND CELEBRATION

One definition of community is giving everything and sharing everything. We have opened up our histories of survival and violence handing them to each other like awkward gifts. Our tears moisten the ground here.

We have lifted each other up, danced each other home, rocked each other into deep laughter. Our bright faces, lit with hope, awaken the leaves.

Both shared mourning and celebration help us grow together.

## 5. WEEDING: MAKING INTENTIONAL SPACE

Gardening is experimental. We want bugs that pollinate but not bugs that eat and kill the plants. We want sun, but we don't want the plants to burn. We want rain, but we don't want the seeds to drown. We want plants to grow but we have to pull up weeds … which are also plants, because they drain resources that our movement needs to grow. UBUNTU's new practice of literally growing gardens together addresses the difficult process of remembering what shared values bring us together now that we have survived the direct conflict of the highly publicized Duke Lacrosse Rape case. While we refuse to participate in the criminalizing agenda of the state and refuse to reinforce divisions between us that serve to weaken our movement, we also have to be vigilant about definition. *I am because we are* can drift into … I am because I'm the best! I am because I'm smarter! I am here because I want the resources this community has earned through struggle even though I don't want to be held accountable by this community. I am around because it seems cool.

We have to define what we want. We want to grow a successful and beautiful garden, which means we have to be explicit about what we are aligned on. No to pesticides and weed-killing chemicals that poison everything. Yes to shared meals and evolving recipes. Since this is a first time process for many of us, we are just learning the difference between the seed we planted as it sprouts up and the weed that threatens to distract us and impoverish our vision. Is the possibility of 501-C3 funding a resource for growth or a weed that undermines the growth of our movement? Is the attention of mass media a tool or an individualistic fuel for our own fame? How do we stop harm within the collective group before it destroys our connections to each other? Do the organizations that make up the coalition sustain the work of UBUNTU, or should individuals involved in UBUNTU be helping to sustain those organizations? What happens when we no longer find committees necessary, but we don't have a committee to revise our statement of purpose to reflect that? How can we affirm a structure that is still in the making? How do we grow the impact of our movement while being very clear about shared values? How do we make spaces for different levels of impact and commitment? How do we differentiate between comrades and allies? Do we have enemies or simply different relationships to power and access?

As the results of our shared action and growth here in Durham, we are now encountering many questions. Lots of things are growing, in many directions ... what is it that will feed us?

## 6. SHARING THE HARVEST

In conclusion, even though we are in an early and tenuous stage of growth, in Durham we know that our survival and our healing is linked to yours. From the beginning of this process (which did not begin with us) we have been committed to sharing our lessons and asking advice far more broadly than our direct communities. Seeds travel. Our growth is connected. The UBUNTU blog (www.iambecauseweare. wordpress.com) and BrokenBeautiful Press (www.brokenbeautiful.wordpress.com) have been ways for us to share the lessons that we are learning with a wider community of survivors, organizers and allies. Our zines including one about *How To Support a Survivor of Sexual Violence*, one about *Moral Revolution*, and our interactive journals and poetic anthologies are in use all over the world. We are honored to have comrades in this process of healing. Noemi Martinez of Hermana Resist in the Rio Grand Valley uses *Blues Record/Improvising Peace* as an anchor in a writing group she facilitates for survivors of gendered violence. Participants in the Allied Media Conference created a zine called *Outlaw Vision: Reclaiming Power, Truth, and Justice for Ourselves* based on the model of UBUNTU's *Wrong is Not My Name* zine.

The Day of Truthtelling, a national event with endorsements and participants from all over the country, has introduced a model of loud, visible, healing-based community response that people around the country have drawn on to respond to the ongoing gendered violence in all of our communities. We are honored that the New York City organizers of a healing vigil to respond to murder of Sanesha Stewart, a young Black trans-woman who was slandered and disrespected in the news media even after her death, were inspired by their participation in and support of the Day of Truthtelling.

We believe that we grow the world we want community by community grounded in our specific contexts but growing a shared and dynamic vision and process that will bloom, revealing alternatives to a violent policing, imprisoning state, and feeding us with the fruits of our loving labor.

**ALEXIS PAULINE GUMBS** *is a queer, Black troublemaker. She works with Critical Resistance, SpiritHouse, Southerners on New Ground, and UBUNTU. She is also the founder of brokenbeautiful press (www.brokenbeautiful.wordpress.com).*

# CAN YOU HEAR

*Anonymous*

Brothers can you hear? Can you hear that voice of reason screaming in your ears? The collective yells of our Ancestors testifying to atrocities perpetuated against the African Nation? Brothers can you hear the blood of your fellow man pleading vengeance for the life lost at the hands of enemy forces? Brother can you or have you been rendered deaf by the constant bombardment of the static noise packaged as music? Have you conditioned your spirit to receive the hard bass line which is followed by words with genocidal intent? Brothers can you hear the cries of the orphaned Black babies whose parents were killed by Black hands. Brothers can you hear the dying gasp of dreams being smothered by foreign Ambitions? Brothers can you hear, can you hear, can you hear? Can you hear what I am asking you? Asking of you? If so, take head and Act!

At the core of the abolitionist position is revolution. The purpose of ridding the state of prisons is to weaken it so destruction is more easily accomplished.

When a state is founded on white supremacy and its policies and logic reflect this hundreds of years later, reform is inadequate as an ends in itself. The logical and appropriate solution is revolution.

I know the abolition of prisons in this country will not happen, at least in my lifetime. So what then is the practical purpose of this position?

Intention. It's to remind practitioners that reform is only a means to an end. It is not enough to have a more humane prison, but to have no prisons. There is no humane white supremacist state. Our actions and our everyday should reflect this.